The Mexican Revolution

The Mexican Revolution

A Short History, 1910–1920

Stuart Easterling

Haymarket Books
Chicago, Illinois

Published by
Haymarket Books
P.O. Box 180165
Chicago, IL 60618
773-583-7884
info@haymarketbooks.org
www.haymarketbooks.org

ISBN: 978-1-60846-182-0

Trade distribution:
In the U.S., Consortium Book Sales and Distribution, www.cbsd.com
In the UK, Turnaround Publisher Services, www.turnaround-uk.com
In Canada, Publishers Group Canada, www.pgcbooks.ca
In Australia, Palgrave Macmillan, www.palgravemacmillan.com.au
All other countries, Publishers Group Worldwide, www.pgw.com

Special discounts are available for bulk purchases by organizations
and institutions. Please contact Haymarket Books for more information
at 773-583-7884 or info@haymarketbooks.org.

This book was published with the generous support of the Wallace
Global Fund and Lannan Foundation.

Library of Congress CIP Data is available.

Contents

List of Illustrations · vii

1. Setting the Stage · 1

Politics and Economics before 1910

Campesinos and Villages before 1910

Mexican Urban Labor before 1910

The Revolution: Many Different Pieces in Motion

2. 1910–1914 · 41

The Spark: Madero's Presidential Campaign

The Unexpected Blaze

The Zapatista Tiger Is Loose

The Death of the Liberal Revolution

The Thug They Had Hoped For

The Rise of Carranza and the Constitutionalists

Pancho Villa: From Bandit to Hero

3. 1914–1920 · 83

The Roots of the Great Revolutionary Split

Obregón and the Revolutionary "Jacobins"

Nationalism and Provincialism in the Revolutionary Camps

Hearts and Minds in Mexico City: Villa and Zapata

Hearts and Minds in Mexico City: Obregón

The Constitutionalists Prevail over Villa

Carranza in Power and the Jacobin Response

Conclusion

Timeline of Major Events   **145**

Acknowledgments   **151**

Notes   **153**

Index   **163**

List of Illustrations

The young Porfirio Díaz   5

The elder Porfirio Díaz   6

Luis Terrazas, Mexico's most powerful landowner   19

Mexican *peón* couple   20

Interior of a wealthy hacienda   21

Mexican pottery workshop   31

Mexican cigarette factory   31

Mine work in Mexico   33

A group of poor women in Mexico City   35

Francisco Madero   42

Madero arriving at a campaign rally   43

Pancho Villa   50

Emiliano Zapata and his officers   52

Anti-Díaz rebels with a makeshift cannon   54

Zapatista recruitment poster   58

Scene in front of Mexico's National Palace
    during the Decena Trágica   65

General Victoriano Huerta and his cabinet   67

Venustiano Carranza   69

Villa and his officers   73

Soldiers of the Northern Division   73

US troops march in Veracruz   79

Pancho Villa reviewing his troops   91

Álvaro Obregón, the Constitutionalist general   97

Álvaro Obregón, the politician   98

Woodcut image of Zapata   123

1

Setting the Stage

It is rare for a hundred-year-old revolution to remain a matter of debate and public controversy. Such is the case with Mexico's revolution of 1910–20, still the most significant event in the nation's modern history.

The anniversary of the Revolution's outbreak, not surprisingly, is widely celebrated each year in Mexico. The official ceremonies pay tribute to its principal leaders: men like Francisco Madero, the idealistic scion of a landowning family, whose call for democracy in Mexico sparked a wider revolt; Emiliano Zapata, the radical agrarian leader who mobilized villagers in the southern state of Morelos and beyond; Pancho Villa, the audacious ex-bandit and popular chieftain from Chihuahua; Venustiano Carranza, the aristocratic state governor turned rebel; and Álvaro Obregón, the brilliant military and political strategist, who in 1920 assumed the presidency after ten years of conflict and popular upheaval.

Yet often overlooked in the celebrations of the great leaders of the past—Madero, Zapata, Villa, Carranza, Obregón—is the fact that all of them bitterly contested one another on the battlefield, and all of them died by the gun rather than in their beds.[1] There is a rich history here, one of popular insurrection, political radicalism, friends turned enemies, and ideals fought for and lost. Understanding the narrative arc of the Mexican Revolution—its causes, process, and outcome—can teach us about far more than just the history of Mexico in the 1910s. Like any revolution, it is a window into understanding human beings and their conflicts.

The Mexican people certainly continue to debate its lessons. There are many Mexicans today who believe that the Revolution's legacy of social reform and grassroots revolt provides a basis for renewing their nation's politics. Such is the view of Andrés Manuel López Obrador, popularly known as AMLO, an opposition political figure and presidential candidate. During the celebrations of the Revolution's centennial in 2010, AMLO declared that the Revolution had shown that the Mexican people "knew how to take on oppressors and tyrants, in order to solve the nation's problems." Moreover, "their sacrifices were not in vain"—the result was Mexico's Constitution of 1917, which enshrined a number of new social reforms: "the right of the peasant to the land; the minimum wage; the right to education; and . . . the ownership and control of the nation over its natural resources." For AMLO and his supporters, these gains have been steadily eroding in recent years.[2]

There are others, however, who believe that the Revolution's legacy is something best left aside. This is the position of one prominent historian, Roger Bartra. On the occasion of winning Mexico's most prestigious historical prize in 2009—just prior to the Revolution's centennial—Bartra argued that the Mexican people should "bury the Revolution." It was high time to recognize that it was "something of the past" and "should not be turned into a source of constant agitation." In addition, the Revolution had "become a conservative idea," according to Bartra, in large part because of how its image was used to justify successive undemocratic governments over the course of decades in Mexico. In this view, the Revolution's principal inheritance was a corrupt and authoritarian regime: the one-party rule by the Institutional Revolutionary Party (PRI) and its predecessors, which dominated Mexican politics for much of the twentieth century.[3]

Another perspective comes from San Pablo Oztotepec, a community in the mountains overlooking the vast sea of lights of Mexico City. A small museum maintained by the town marks the site where the Plan de Ayala—the radical agrarian manifesto of Zapata and his followers—was ratified. The town's residents, young and old, can tell the story of their allegiance to Zapata, and of how Carranza's troops later came to the village to burn their crops and homes. Their independence continues to this day: San Pablo admits no chain stores, bars, or hotels within its boundaries. The community is very tight-knit, and captured thieves are lucky to escape the town with their lives. During the anniversary celebrations of the Revolution, young girls dress as Adelitas—the women who served in the revolutionary armies—and young boys don the garb of Zapatista soldiers: white pajamas (the traditional attire of the agricultural laborer), child-sized cartridge belts, wooden rifles, sombreros, and painted-on Zapata mustaches. To "bury the Revolution" and its memory in San Pablo today would not be a simple proposition.

AMLO, Roger Batra, and the people of San Pablo Oztotepec are all particular examples, but their views and experience reflect broad currents of contemporary opinion in Mexico. The point is that Revolution's legacy remains a contested one. This is even more so given that profound changes in Mexico since the 1980s—collectively referred to as neoliberalism—have undone much of what the Revolution wrought. Indeed, one could argue that in spite of the annual celebrations of the Revolution and its heroes, the results of the decade of the 1980s now weigh heavier on Mexican society than those of the 1910s. This book cannot address all of these issues, nor can it untangle the nature of the Revolution's legacy for the present day. But it hopes to provide an understanding of the conflicts of that tumultuous decade for the reader, and an opportunity for further thinking about the questions they raise.

Politics and Economics before 1910

Prior to the outbreak of revolution, the most important figure in Mexican politics by far was the nation's long-standing president, Porfirio Díaz. A popular military hero in his youth, Díaz came to power in 1876 at the head of an army revolt following more than thirty years of civil war and foreign invasion in Mexico. During his long rule—known as the Porfiriato—Díaz and his allies sought to create a powerful central government that the country had previously lacked, and to place Mexico on the path of modern capitalist economic development. This meant putting an end to the political instability, armed conflict, and popular upheaval that had

The young
Porfirio Díaz

characterized much of the country's nineteenth-century history. In particular, Díaz made it his goal to contain and repress the country's long tradition of rural and agrarian revolt.[4] Díaz accomplished all this by means of a political dictatorship, one that was increasingly heavy-handed in its use of repression as the years went by.

The elder Porfirio Díaz

One clear outcome of the Díaz regime was a massive economic boom that radically transformed Mexico. Over the course of his rule (1876–1910), total railroad track in the country expanded from 640 kilometers to nearly 20,000. Exports increased by a factor of six, averaging a growth rate of more than 6 percent per year. Boom towns appeared almost overnight: Cananea, for example, in the northern state of Sonora, was a village of one hundred people in

1891; by 1906 it was a bustling mining center of some twenty-five thousand, producing 10 percent of Mexico's mineral output. Increased commerce meant that the total money in circulation in Mexico increased twelvefold in thirty years, from 25 million pesos in 1880 to more than 300 million in 1910. By 1895, Mexico's government had a budget surplus for the first time. Foreign investment also soared, increasing from 110 million pesos in 1884 to 3.4 billion pesos in 1911, with the United States (mining and railroads), Britain (petroleum), and France (banks) as the largest investors. And by 1911 Mexico was ranked as the third-largest oil producer in the world, with an annual production of 14 million barrels.[5]

It was a transformation unprecedented in Mexican history: the country was increasingly, and rapidly, integrated into the north Atlantic capitalist world. Meanwhile, Mexico's most powerful landowners and businessmen were extremely grateful to Díaz for the political stability and economic expansion that came with his regime. Put simply, his government allowed them to acquire wealth on an unprecedented scale, and equally important, it allowed them to keep it. In December 1905, five years before the outbreak of revolution, Mexico's pliant Congress would present the dictator with a jewel-encrusted medallion in an elaborate ceremony. It bore the words "He Pacified and Unified the Nation."[6]

Another important result of this period of economic expansion was a significant growth in Mexico's rural and urban middle classes. These included educated professionals such as lawyers and journalists; commercial traders, shop owners, and merchants; entrepreneurial ranchers and farmers who held enough land to make a living selling their produce; and skilled artisans and other self-employed producers of goods and services. People such as these survived and advanced—or expected to—by means of their education, skills, and commercial acumen. They were often highly ambitious, and believed that they should rise above their peers due to their personal efforts.

Yet while the Porfirian system had created this growing new segment of society, it also effectively shut them out. How did it do this? Mexico's rapidly expanding economy had certainly concentrated wealth at the top. But the key was that the Porfirian state helped ensure that the same politically influential people at the top always benefited from economic boom times and were sheltered during times of crisis. As a result, the middle classes were largely prevented from attaining the kind of wealth and influence that was increasingly visible in Mexican society, or even from attaining the level that they felt they deserved.

The Mexican Revolution has often been associated with demands related to the land, and in particular agrarian reform—redistributing land held by the rich to the poor. This view is entirely correct, as we'll see. But the aspiring and increasingly angry middle classes, or those who shared their outlook, also placed their stamp on the politics and course of the Revolution. Commercially minded landowners and ranchers, for example, as well as people involved in petty trade or mercantile activity, were kept from advancing, or even surviving, given the tremendous political power of the very rich. The educated middle class—intellectuals, journalists, lawyers, and the like—were denied the political voice and influence that they believed corresponded to the extent of their education and learning. The Porfirian state functioned in various ways to create this state of affairs. The principal reasons included widespread political corruption and privilege, the abuse of political power, and a lack of local political autonomy.

We can take up the issue of political privilege and corruption first. In short, those with access to people in government—whether through friendship, family connections, commercial links, or bribery—made out far better than those who did not. This may sound like an unremarkable observation, common to all governments to some degree. But the degree to which it existed in Porfirian Mexico was massive, and it generated profound and widespread resentment. In any legal dispute, for example, judges could invariably be expected to issue a decision that benefited the nephew of a government minister, or the cousin of a state senator, or the son of a municipal president. Indeed, merely challenging such influential people could land you in jail. Moreover, the disputes that arose with moneyed political insiders were not necessarily trivial ones. Take losing a legal battle over access to water from a river: it might not just mean that the losers did with less; it could mean that the losers were utterly ruined. These sorts of political advantages, and their consequences, could be found at all levels of the Porfirian system.

Another egregious example for contemporaries was taxation. Debates over who should bear the burden of taxation, and to what degree, also characterize all modern societies. But in Porfirian Mexico the wealthy, including large landowners and other powerful businessmen, enjoyed tax privileges that were widely regarded as highly unfair and embittered many people. Indeed, political connections and avoidance of taxes often went hand in hand. This meant, of course, that the burden rested on everyone else. It was said, for example, that the vegetable vendors in the city of Guanajuato paid more in taxes than all the landowners in the surrounding region. Another case was the state of Chihuahua—Pancho Villa's base of operations—where property taxes were officially regressive, operating to the marked disadvantage of those with smaller land-holdings. On top of this, taxes had increased eightfold in the two decades before the Revolution.[7] The fact that the state government had become the personal fiefdom of the Terrazas family, Mexico's largest landowners, only added fuel to the fire.

The second factor mentioned above was the issue of abuse of political power. This went far beyond questions of bribery or favoritism. During the dictatorship, government authorities at all levels consistently made use of their positions for the purpose of private gain, usually at the expense of those who were not already political insiders or the well-off. The Porfirian *jefes políticos*, the appointed local political officials, were especially despised for this reason. One contemporary described this figure as "the local authority of the central government, the boss of the town and often its moneylender, pawnbroker, house agent, merchant and marriage broker at the same time, and all greatly to his own profit."[8] They often enriched themselves not only through control over commercial activity, but also through extortion—via arbitrary "taxes" and "fines"—directed at shaking down nearly all sectors of the population, be they small farmers, shop owners, tradespeople, or poor townsfolk. But perhaps their most feared authority, one typically used against dissidents and troublemakers, was that of deportation to the Yucatán peninsula. There the victim would be forced to work in the slave-like conditions of the henequen plantations—another booming Porfirian export business—which often meant an early death. Some *jefes políticos* even turned this into a lucrative business, shipping off the indigents and drunks that ended up in local jails in return for cash payments from the planters.[9]

In short, national politics was a dictatorship, and so was nearly every state and town. As one revolutionary leader later observed of this arrangement, "I began to feel the need for change in our social organization when I was 19, when, back in my town . . . I saw the police commissioner get drunk almost every day in the town pool hall, in the company of his secretary; with the local judge who was also the . . . tax collector; with the head of the post office; and with some merchant or army officer, persons all of whom constituted the influential class of that small world."[10] This may sound like small-town politics to some, but Mexico at this time was a country of small towns and villages. If you crossed the people in the local "influential class," they could ruin your life, and your family's. And if they had, you might well be among those who took up arms across Mexico with the outbreak of revolution.

Lastly, there was the issue of local political autonomy. Mexico's nineteenth-century Liberals, who designed the country's 1857 constitution, had placed great emphasis on political federalism, meaning the devolution of power to the states and local municipal control. This doctrine had considerable grassroots appeal: rural and provincial Mexicans had long valued the ability to manage their own local affairs, without interference from powerful outsiders.[11] The Porfirian dictatorship, however, in constructing the most far-reaching centralized state in the country's history, ran roughshod over this ideal. State governors and local officials (such as the highly unpopular jefes políticos) were subject to approval from the national executive, often from Díaz himself, when they were not simply imposed. Once in power, as we have seen, they benefited their limited circle of friends, and typically ignored—or punished—everyone else. Meanwhile, people among the lower and middle social classes were subject to increasing and arbitrary taxation from afar with little visible benefit in their localities, and certainly with no political representation. Young men were subject to the feared and hated *leva*, that is, forced recruitment into the national army, which was often nothing more than a ticket to hunger and disease.

And so when the opportunity presented itself in 1910, these combined political factors—privilege and corruption, abuse of political power, and a lack of local autonomy—would produce armed revolt on their own, even in the absence of agrarian demands. Most significantly, they would produce revolt that united people across different social classes against the power of the central government; this point is key for understanding the course of the Revolution.[12]

A poor rural family, for example, could easily be devastated by the loss of one of their able-bodied sons (or worse, the father) to the *leva*. A village shop owner would resent having to provide goods on indefinite credit to the local jefe político, his relatives, and his cronies; not to do so might mean going to jail. An ambitious mule-driver could be driven out of business when his trade route was coveted, and taken, by a friend or crony of a state government official. An educated journalist or lawyer could lose the ability to practice his profession merely by crossing the wrong people. A small rancher would resent increased taxes, which, in his eyes, went to pay for banquets in the state capital or Mexico City rather than new roads—and he was probably not far from the truth. Such taxation would be even more galling when his larger and better-connected competitors seemed to pay no taxes at all. All this combined to form a deep cross-class resentment of the central government, and a desire to get rid of its influence. The loudest dissent, as we shall see, came from the booming states of the Mexican north, which bordered the United States: Sonora (home to Obregón), Chihuahua (home to Pancho Villa), and Coahuila (home to Madero and Carranza).[13]

In the face of such deep and widespread dissatisfaction, the problem the Porfirian regime faced was that it was unable to change with the times. The strong hand of Díaz, and the powerful state he created, had kept in check the conflicts and revolts that had typified nineteenth-century Mexican history. But his centralized and corrupt political system became extremely rigid and inflexible. It was unable to do away with the aforementioned abuses and tyranny that characterized it throughout, especially since these abuses benefited so many people in government. Furthermore, they appeared to keep society in some semblance of order, meaning an order that benefited Mexico's most wealthy and politically connected people. The Porfirian system may have suppressed conflict for a time, and created the conditions that made Mexico's economic transformation possible. Yet it would not allow the ambitious and growing middle classes—or, eventually, even disaffected members of the landlord class—a space to express themselves politically and reform the system peacefully from within.

Specifically, the lack of democracy in Mexico meant the state did not allow for a renewal or turnover of its personnel, through elections or other means, even when loyal critics thought it extremely necessary. Although few among the middle classes had a desire to carry out radical change, as political outsiders they were repeatedly frustrated in their efforts to make adjustments to the Porfirian political and economic system. Their most prominent attempt to encourage reform was the widespread formation of so-called Liberal clubs starting around the turn of the century. They focused on trying to restore the norms of the cherished Constitution of 1857, and to advance a program of moderate social reform. Yet their lobbying and criticisms of the government were frequently met with arrests and repression.[14]

So how did the system work, as the Revolution approached? At the very top of the regime stood Porfirio Díaz, who had historically administered it in a direct, personal, hands-on manner. Indeed, it has been said of the US political system that it was built by geniuses to be run by idiots; the Porfirian system was also painstakingly built by a political genius—Díaz himself—but it required a genius to run it. Díaz possessed intimate knowledge of the coalitions and deal-making going on in states and even towns across the country, and was frequently involved in them directly. But as he aged—he was eighty at the outbreak of revolution—the vigor and acumen with which he had ruled the country were in decline. The same was true of the Porfirian ministers, senators, and governors: the average age of these men was seventy years, whereas only 8 percent of Mexicans were over fifty years old. Four men in Díaz's cabinet, in fact, had held their posts for twenty-nine years or longer; state governors also typically held office for absurdly long periods. In short, it was very difficult for new blood to break in to the system, and especially for a younger generation of ambitious middle-class reformers. As one of these men put it, the Porfirian political system was dominated by "mummies that materially obstruct our march towards progress."[15]

The worst of these mummies were likely the *científicos* (scientists), a term used for the elite cabal of advisers and administrators around President Díaz. They had close ties to the nation's

financial and banking elite, and held strongly to an ideology of enlightened expert administration. For them the business of politics
and running society was a science, albeit one that could be carried
out only by select "scientists" such as themselves. Democracy would
lead to bad—or "unscientific"—outcomes because of the ignorance
of the public. They thus held the public, and particularly the lower
classes, in considerable contempt. This contempt, however, was increasingly reciprocated: well before the Revolution, *científico* had
become a dirty word. They were widely seen as the pinnacle of
Porfirian elite domination and arrogance. When Mexico's economy faced repeated crises in the last years of Diaz's rule, their
image lost its luster even further.

Thus by 1910 President Díaz and his advisers—in spite of
their elevated self-estimation—were increasingly regarded as being
unable to administer Mexico's now highly complex society. More
specifically, they could not do so in the interests of all members of
the economic elite, much less the frustrated middle classes. Political
democracy became a burning issue, and when Francisco Madero
launched his presidential campaign, and later his revolt, many in
the middle classes rallied to his banner, which he undoubtedly expected. An unexpected and undesired consequence, however, was
that the rural poor rallied to his banner as well, and on a massive
scale. It was their grievances and demands that radicalized the
course of the Revolution. We now turn to their plight.

Campesinos and Villages before 1910

A dictatorship can come to an end without widespread revolutionary upheaval. Indeed, if the only source of conflict in Porfirian

Mexico was the political and economic grievances of the middle classes, the revolts that broke out in 1910 would have been far easier to contain or make concessions to. However, a crucial second factor behind the outbreak of revolution was the deteriorating conditions faced by many of Mexico's rural campesinos under Díaz.* The Mexican Revolution was, above all, driven by agrarian grievances and mass agrarian mobilization. Middle-class social reformers and discontented landowners may have started things off, but what made the Mexican Revolution such an intractable conflict was the question of land for campesinos and their villages.

In spite of all the major socioeconomic changes under Díaz, Mexico remained a rural and agrarian society: 80 percent of the population lived in communities of fewer than five thousand inhabitants, and nearly 70 percent dedicated themselves to agriculture.[16] Meanwhile, over the course of the Porfirian dictatorship the conflict between villages and the *hacienda*, the landed estate, became more and more contentious, polarized, and bitter. Some of these agrarian disputes had gone on for generations; children in the village would be raised with a consciousness of the conflict and its history. One

---

* A brief clarification of terminology is necessary at this point. The term *campesino* (literally, country person) is preferred here to *peasant* principally because many Mexican villagers were not peasants in the strict sense of the word, meaning rural subsistence smallholders. Some, a shrinking number, were indeed smallholders growing corn, squash, beans, and chiles on their own lands for their family; others were sharecroppers or renters on the property of a local landlord; others performed seasonal agricultural labor for the landlord with little more than a garden plot of their own; still others produced anything from honey to reed baskets to charcoal for sale using the little bit of land they or their village still held. Many families engaged in some combination of these activities. What many campesinos often shared, however, was a desire to till land of their own, both for subsistence and for commerce.

such conflict in the north-central state of Querétaro, for example, was finally settled in 1879 after going on for 318 years.[17]

Key changes during Díaz's rule tipped the balance sharply in favor of large landowners, however. First was the effect of the railroad, and the access to expanded domestic and international markets that came with it. This set off a massive land boom—or more precisely, a land grab—in rural Mexico. The possibilities for gain "dazzled landed elites," in the words of historian John Tutino.[18] Second, Díaz gave these landed elites every opportunity to profit: in 1883 a law was passed permitting easy acquisition of so-called *terrenos baldíos*, that is, unoccupied or unused lands. Any private company that surveyed these lands was entitled to a third of them, and the right to purchase the remaining two-thirds from the government at rock-bottom prices. The only thing that could stop this process was an official title of ownership, something few rural villagers had. Even when they did, the landowners' attorneys often found ways to invalidate their dusty old documents.

When villagers could not produce a title to their common lands—including woodlands, water sources, mule paths, or pasture that they had used for generations—they were easily taken away by aggressive landlords, backed by the force of law. Barbed wire would go up soon after, fencing off what the village had always regarded as its own and often depended on for basic subsistence as well as commercial activity. It should be noted, moreover, that these measures were not always carried out by some distant wealthy landowner. In certain cases, an enterprising member of the locality—perhaps an ally of the jefe político, or of some other local authority figure, such as the priest—would take the same steps, enriching himself as a result and generating vast pools of resentment within the community.[19]

The overall effects of this process were stunning. During the Díaz regime thirty-nine million hectares of untitled land, about a fifth of Mexico's total land area, equivalent in size to the state of California, were converted into private property. Much of it was highly concentrated in terms of ownership, and some also went to foreign interests: 547,000 hectares in northern Mexico, for example, became the sole possession of the Richardson Construction Company in Los Angeles. The newspaper tycoon William Randolph Hearst also acquired a large estate for himself in the state of Chihuahua, one measuring 350,000 hectares, that is, a property of 1,351 square miles, or more than four times the size of New York City's five boroughs. But these were not even the biggest players in the land grab: one Mexican investor, for example, obtained properties of more than one million hectares; another domestic investment group acquired lands exceeding two million hectares. The king of them all, however, was undoubtedly Luis Terrazas, the Chihuahuan magnate and perhaps the largest landowner in all of Latin America. Among his many business enterprises, he owned roughly fifty haciendas and ranches, totaling nearly three million hectares in all.[20] It was said that when Terrazas was asked if he was from Chihuahua—"¿Eres de Chihuahua?"—he would respond "No, Chihuahua es mía" (No, Chihuahua is mine).[21]

As a result of this process, in many parts of Mexico the hacienda became practically the only source of arable land or employment. By 1910, roughly half of all rural Mexicans are estimated to live or labor on the haciendas. In certain regions this figure was even higher: in the north-central state of Zacatecas, for example, it was 76 percent; in the state of San Luis Potosí, it was 82 percent.[22] Some people became *peones acasillados*, that is, resident laborers and

Luis Terrazas, Mexico's most powerful landowner

servants on the hacienda, completely dependent on the estate for their basic survival. The estate's *peones* would receive a meager wage, along with a small plot and a roof over their heads, in exchange for their labor, personal services, and loyalty to the landlord. In some cases they were paid not in cash but in scrip that had to be spent at

Mexican *peón* couple

Interior of a wealthy hacienda

the *tienda de raya*, the landlord's monopolistic "company store." Corporal punishment, including whippings, was not uncommon, but likely the most feared punishment for the *peón* was to be evicted from the hacienda entirely. The hacienda also housed a smaller number of more skilled and mobile workers, including cowboys, ranch hands, mechanics, and the like. The residents on a large estate usually numbered a few hundred people.

The poor conditions notwithstanding, landlords would often make a show of paternalism toward their residents. As one *hacendado* (landlord) noted at the time, the peones expected that he be "a sort of living providence to supplement and relieve the shortcomings of their own improvidence."[23] And so some landlords might give out articles of clothing or candy upon returning to their estate following time spent at their home in the city. Others might house a chapel on their property, occasionally visited by a priest, where the landlord could graciously pay for baptisms and weddings. In the case of a particularly loyal resident, the hacendado might agree to be the godfather of a child. A graveyard would also be available on the estate, where the peones often met an early death, but at least received a dignified burial.

The life of resident peones was far from comfortable, but it was assumed that if they remained under the landlord's protection, at least their families would be relatively secure. For this reason, the most desperate or dependent peones were not likely to rebel against their masters. That said, as the opportunities for profit grew during the Porfiriato, and as new investors took over many haciendas, the old paternalistic practices were often reduced or eliminated. One hacienda in Durango, for example, ceased providing a bull each year for a local village festival, and later even stopped providing candles for its chapel, in the interest of saving money. These sorts of changes helped worsen the image of the hacendado among estate residents and village campesinos.[24]

Village campesinos, who did not live on the hacienda property, had a different relationship to the estate. A key factor was the loss of village lands: with little or no land of their own, campesinos often became renters, sharecroppers, or occasional day laborers on the hacienda.* In the landlord's relations with these people it becomes clear that he cannot be described as simply a magnanimous

---

* A sharecropper rented a landlord's land, paying with a portion of his harvest; a renter typically paid in cash; a day laborer received wages for seasonal planting and harvesting work. At times these roles overlapped, as when a sharecropper (or his sons) would try to find work as a day laborer on the estate as well.

and paternalistic feudal baron. Rather, he was an aggressive and diversified capitalist entrepreneur, who ruled over "a productive enterprise capable of turning plants into money," in the words of historian Arturo Warman.[25] Sharecroppers and renters were often the greatest source of profits on the hacienda; moreover, given the landlords' monopoly on arable land, these tenants were frequently subject to whatever terms the landlords set.

As economic opportunities and competition expanded significantly in the years before 1910, the landlords' business strategies produced sharper and sharper conflicts between them and their tenants in many parts of Mexico. Be they successful or struggling, landlords used sharecroppers and renters to minimize their own risk, moving them about like factors of production and thus making their lives progressively more insecure. The landlord would shift to demanding crops, cash, or labor for payment as it suited him; he would regularly revise contracts and demand more production from tenants; he would push them to more marginal lands; he would offer them seasonal wage labor as a fallback option, but only when the market was favorable.[26] Tenants on haciendas thus lacked the security of stable employment or the independence that came with owning one's own land. Day laborers faced this same problem, often having to line up at the hacienda gates at dawn, desperately hoping to be selected for work. Those who were overly troublesome were locked out from working or renting on the hacienda entirely; at times this policy would even encompass entire villages.

In short, one could say that insult was increasingly heaped upon injury. One estate manager in the Laguna region, in a notable understatement, remarked that the hacienda system had "lent itself throughout to the abuses that led to the Revolution."[27] Indeed, the

Laguna—a productive agricultural territory where the northern states of Coahuila and Durango meet—would become a hotbed of revolutionary upheaval after 1910.

The ranks of the Revolution's armies would thus include many hacienda day laborers, sharecroppers, and renters. But the base of the agrarian revolution was in the villages, and especially the so-called free villages, that is, those that still retained some of their lands and a precarious independence. Residents of these villages were often the ones who most resisted and resented the hacienda's growth and domination. Many of them had witnessed, over the course of their lifetime, the painful shift from independent landholding to sharecropping or wage labor on the hacienda.

Although life in these communities was neither egalitarian nor without conflict, they provided their residents with a basis for collective organization, and often a history of collective solidarity, against the landlords. This was even more so in the villages that practiced a form of communal landownership, where land could not be sold, and was distributed or assigned to residents by the village leadership. It was these communities that provided the basis for the Zapatista movement, the most intransigent and unbreakable of the revolutionary forces. In its home state of Morelos, as well as in neighboring ones, rapidly expanding commercial agriculture (in this case, sugar production) collided with long-standing villages, many of which held land communally. The results were ultimately explosive, both in Morelos and in other parts of Mexico.

The extent and polarization of these conflicts can be better understood when we look at particular examples. Many villages faced near-extinction in the years before 1910. The village of

Naranja—a community of Tarascan-speakers in one of the valleys of rural Michoacán—is one such case. Here a neighboring marsh had for generations provided the villagers with a source of fish and game birds, as well as reeds to weave into baskets for sale in nearby towns. But with the coming of the railroad, a group of outside entrepreneurs (and their lawyers) arrived on the scene and petitioned the government to survey and purchase the "unoccupied" lands around Naranja. The villagers protested, but could not produce an official title, and they lost access to the marsh: it was drained and became part of the new landowner's fields. Villagers, if they were lucky, were able to sharecrop on the hacienda's most marginal and infertile lands; others were forced to walk two days to the lowlands to find work as gang laborers on plantations. Many of them, not surprisingly, would develop into agrarian revolutionaries.[28]

Another case was the village of Villa de Carbonera, in the center-north state of San Luis Potosí. The owner of the local hacienda, which completely surrounded the village, had decided to resurvey his property. When the survey was complete he placed his new boundary markers, and in the process helped himself to 875 acres of communal grazing land belonging to the village. The villagers went to court and, using their land titles, demonstrated that the land belonged to them. The boundary markers were moved. But the change didn't matter: the landowner had a close friend in Porfirio Diaz's cabinet. He simply moved the boundary markers once again, this time accompanied by Mexican army troops. The new boundaries were then rubber-stamped at the highest levels of government. The heirs to the hacienda would continue their father's usurpation of village lands, up to the eve of the Revolution. Meanwhile, a respected local family, the Cedillos, had long lived in the shadow of this notorious hacienda. Three of its sons would become prominent agrarian revolutionaries after 1910.[29]

But Naranja and Villa de Carbonera were probably among the more fortunate villages facing the land grab that took place in rural Mexico. During this process whole communities were often literally swallowed up. In many parts of Mexico, the landlord's property began at the spot where the last village street ended. One hacienda in the state of Hidalgo, for example, held twenty-two villages within its boundaries. The community of Tepalcingo, in Morelos, was completely surrounded by a stone wall several miles long, built by a local landlord without consulting the townsfolk. Residents of San José de Gracia, in Durango, would regularly walk past a hacienda boundary stone that rested at the foot of the church tower.

Many of these villages caught in the hacienda's web—with little or no land, pasture, or water resources of their own—would stagnate, if not disappear entirely. At times the elimination was completely deliberate. The centuries-old village of Tequisquitengo, for example, also in Morelos, had been locked in a legal battle with an hacienda over the use of a river. The landlord ultimately chose to dam the river and deliberately flood the town. When the job was finished, only the church spire showed above the waters.[30] The sense of desperation, humiliation, and rage felt by the villagers of Tequisquitengo and others like them must be kept in mind when one considers why so many people joined the revolutionary armies after 1910. One hacienda administrator captured this sentiment well, describing the campesinos as people who had been "persecuted viciously to the slow and brooding growth of vindictive hate that at last bursts forth in revolution."[31]

Yet Mexico's rulers seemed oblivious to the gathering storm. One prominent landlord in Morelos, for example, informed of the campesinos' grievances immediately prior to the outbreak of revolution, famously responded by saying "Let them farm in a flowerpot"—a declaration surely as well received as Marie Antoinette's "let them eat cake" was in France.[32] It is worth noting, moreover, that our Morelos landlord and the científicos were not the only members of the Porfirian upper crust who disdained the lower classes. A widespread view among the elite was that the plight of the poor was due to their own laziness, vice, and stupidity. This perspective was frequently extended to the nation's indigenous ("Indian") population as well. Also popular was social Darwinism, which held that the poor were merely individuals who had failed at the "survival of the fittest."[33] The "fittest," naturally, were the members of the Porfirian upper class: the landlords, bankers, and wealthy businessmen. The fact that a poor campesino was to be found at the bottom of society merely demonstrated that he had earned such a position.

These explanations increasingly did not fit reality as many people saw it, however. Who had benefited from the boom times of the Porfiriato—and who had not—was widely seen as having little to do with merit. There were those in the middle class who strongly believed they had been barred from acquiring wealth and influence—as the closed circle of the very rich and politicians clearly had—or from even earning a secure living, in spite of their own "fitness" or effort. Few campesinos could accept that they deserved their lot when they had lost their land and livelihood to legal maneuvers undertaken by a powerful landowner. The vast wealth and territory concentrated in the hands of the elite came to be widely seen as illegitimate—that is, acquired by means of entrenched political privilege, corruption, and violence rather than honest work. Indeed, the villagers of Hueyapan in the state of Morelos believed that no good could come of money earned on the neighboring hacienda because the landlord's wealth had come through a secret pact with the Devil.[34] Given these outlooks, when the Revolution broke out, the rich would be frequent targets of retribution. The members of Porfirian high society were often stunned to discover the anger and resentment that existed among their "inferiors."

In the countryside, the landlord and his estate were undoubtedly the greatest target of this anger. Its extent should not be underestimated if one is to understand the course of the Revolution. The revolutionary decade of 1910–20 was, at its core, a sustained mass assault on the haciendas and their owners, one that continued long after the Revolution was officially declared over. As soon as the opportunity presented itself, campesinos across the country acted on their bitterness and rage, attacking estates in various parts of the country, distributing their land without waiting for official sanction, and recovering access to the forest, pasture, and water that they had lost. They joined revolutionary armies and smaller bands, fighting for land, revenge, and in some cases merely booty from the rich. Towns and cities in Mexico were soon crowded with landlords who had fled the countryside in fear. Even in regions where grassroots land distribution did not take place, popular armed bandits roamed at will, robbing the estates, shooting landlords and hacienda managers despised by local villagers, and at times even razing the landlord's buildings to the ground. Take one such hacienda, in the state of Durango: according to a fawning contemporary, it was a "magnificent country estate . . . furnished in regal style and containing many priceless old paintings."[35] It was blown up by rebels with dynamite.

Mexican Urban Labor before 1910

Having considered the grievances and politics of both Mexico's middle classes and campesinos, it is now appropriate to turn to a third actor in the revolutionary drama: the Mexican urban worker. The process of rapid economic development under Porfirio Díaz beginning in the 1890s had created the first significant industrial working class in Mexico. Railroad workers, for example, had not existed before the creation and expansion of the industry, but by 1910 they numbered in the tens of thousands.* The arrival of the streetcar in a number of major Mexican cities created another skilled working-class occupation that did not exist before. In the two decades before the outbreak of the Revolution a modern textile sector also emerged, reaching a total of thirty-four thousand workers, many concentrated in large factories producing cloth for domestic consumption. Mining, a boom-and-bust industry that dated from the colonial period, recovered and expanded considerably thanks to the railroads. In 1910 miners, living in mining camps and towns found largely in the Mexican north, numbered almost a hundred thousand. More generally, various mass consumer goods such as soap, candles, beer, furniture, soft drinks, cigarettes, meat, and baked goods were increasingly shifting to small-scale factory production.[36]

---

*The railroad also played an important role in opening markets for other industries: the cost of shipping a ton of cotton from Mexico City to the provinces, for example, declined from sixty-one dollars to three dollars over the course of Díaz's rule.

In many areas the expansion of a working-class labor force happened extremely quickly. The dramatic growth of the mining town of Cananea has already been mentioned; another case was the town of Torreón, a crucial railroad hub in the Laguna region, which grew from about two hundred people in 1892 to thirty-four thousand in 1910. But in relative terms the Mexican working class was still small: workers in "industrial occupations" (which included mining and manufacturing) represented 16 percent of the labor force, and this category still included large numbers of artisanal laborers. So while the expansion of the working class was rapid, the concentration of production (shifting from small shops to mechanized factories) and the proletarianization of artisanal labor (converting independent artisans into wage workers) were nonetheless historically still at their inception.

A comparison may help to illustrate this point. As mentioned, Mexico had thirty-four thousand textile factory workers in 1910. But it also had forty-four thousand shoemakers, twenty-three thousand potters, twenty-three thousand mat-weavers, and eighteen thousand hatmakers. These mostly worked in artisan shops and family businesses, or on a "putting out" basis, laboring in their homes for a buyer rather than in factories. In some industries, such as textiles, the artisan had largely been displaced by factory production. In others, such as shoemaking, the process was still under way in the years before 1910. In still others, such as mat-weaving, which produced a fairly universal consumer item in Mexico, production remained on a smaller, nonindustrial scale.[37]

Reflecting this ongoing transition, Mexican labor organizations had historically been based in artisanal traditions, and were focused on mutual aid, self-improvement, and the formation of cooperatives,

Mexican pottery workshop

Mexican cigarette factory

rather than on direct confrontations and strikes against employers. Mass trade unionism was a relatively recent phenomenon, in many cases successfully emerging only in the ten years before the outbreak of revolution in 1910. Many of these early trade unions largely focused on economic and workplace issues, but political currents could also be found within them; this included anarcho-syndicalism, which developed in Mexico in part through the influence of immigrants from Spain. A number of middle-class reformers in the Liberal camp also became anarchists and agitated for radical change and strike action. But the most widespread doctrine among workers critical of the Porfirian establishment remained the Mexican Liberal tradition, with its emphasis on inalienable rights, including freedom of association (which for workers included the right to organize unions), and democratic, constitutional government.[38]

In general, conditions for Mexican workers in this era were grim. Workdays of twelve hours, and at times sixteen hours, were the norm. The wages of a textile worker or miner were higher than those of the rural peones, but their lives were often not appreciably better. Workers in these two important industries frequently labored in dictatorial company towns, and textile workers were—like the peones—subject to the *tienda de raya* and the payment of part of their wages in scrip. Numerous "fines" imposed by managers, for breaking workplace regulations, cut into their wages. In one textile factory workers even had to pay a weekly commission to feed the company dogs. Further undermining workers' incomes was a dramatic rise in the prices of basic food staples in the last decade of Porfirian rule.

Industrial labor, meanwhile, was extremely unsafe. Miners were especially at risk, and received little or no compensation in

Mine work in Mexico

the case of death or injury. When a miner died, a company might limit itself to paying for a pine box to bury him in. In another case, when seventy miners died in a blast in Coahuila in 1910, the mining company paid their widows the equivalent of two weeks' wages. Miners were also susceptible to the wild fluctuations of the international market for minerals, and thus had little job security: in the three years before the Revolution, in fact, mass layoffs devastated the mining industry in the north.[39] Many of these unemployed workers would end up in Pancho Villa's armies.

To the conditions of work one must add the conditions of urban life for workers and the poor. Those that did not live in company towns ended up in the rapidly expanding and squalid cities of the Porfirian era. Mexico City was one example: a glittering jewel for the rich, and purgatory at best for the poor, with the middle classes looking downward with fear and upward with envy. The capital had nearly doubled in size between 1890 and 1910 as displaced rural people flooded into cities across the country. The urban poor typically lived in cramped conditions with no running water, plumbing, or garbage disposal; one survey of a working-class area in Mexico City found that people on average lived, or just slept, seven to a room. A prolabor newspaper, *El México Obrero*, caustically noted that the bathrooms of the rich were more hygienic than the living quarters of workers in the capital.

As a result of these conditions, diseases such as typhus were rampant. The death rate for Mexico City was the second highest in the country (only the semi-slave plantation region of the Yucatán exceeded it), and higher than the rates for large cities in other developing countries, such as Madras and Cairo. Adding to this was the incidence of crime: the rate of murder doubled, and of robbery

A group of poor women in Mexico City

tripled, in the ten years before 1910. It was no surprise that the influential newspaper *El País* referred to the working-class districts of the capital as "centers of sickness and death." Urban life, and especially life for workers and the poor, was thus more and more insecure and desperate toward the end of the Porfirian dictatorship.[40]

In this overall environment workers increasingly turned to strike action to better their conditions. In the four decades from 1865 to 1905, textile workers led the way with a total of seventy-one strikes; on the railways there were twenty-five; the mines followed with seventeen; and tobacco workers carried out fifteen. None of these indicate a high density of strike activity over the bulk of the dictatorship. After 1905, however, strikes were progressively more numerous and militant in certain industries, and helped undermine the legitimacy of the regime. Strikes by textile workers in 1906–11, for example, exceeded the total of the previous forty years, clearly alarming the authorities.

Mexico's Porfirian rulers had kept a close eye on the state of Mexico's nascent industries, which they saw as the basis for the country's future economic development. But they did little to improve workers' conditions, and as time went on Díaz was ever more likely to respond to labor dissent with direct and bloody repression. In the eyes of many middle-class social reformers, meanwhile, the solution was modern labor legislation—an eight-hour day, restrictions on child labor, and even the right to organize—so that Mexican capitalism, and particularly Mexican industrial capitalism, could take a step forward and avoid the destructive conflicts that were clearly on the rise.

Undoubtedly the two most prominent strikes of the Díaz era were those among miners in Cananea, Sonora, in 1906 and among textile workers in the "textile corridor" states of Puebla, Orizaba, and Veracruz in 1907. Both strikes were politically significant because of where they took place. The first hit the largest mining center in the country, which employed seventy-five hundred workers; the second involved six thousand workers, striking multiple factories, in what was considered one of the country's most modern industries: textiles. In both cases wages were relatively high by Mexican standards, and were not the sole or principal factor behind strike action. In Cananea, a town close to the US border, a number of workers had been exposed to anarcho-syndicalist ideas by Mexican radicals in exile, as well as by the Western Federation of Miners in the US Southwest. Among their demands were the elimination of wage differentials between Mexican and North American workers, an eight-hour day, and the dismissal of abusive foremen. In the case of the textile workers, strike action took place after employers universally introduced new dictatorial regulations in their mills. The initial walkout shut down some thirty factories, an indication of the growing extent of labor organization in the industry. Indeed, the textile strike of 1907 was perhaps Mexico's first mass strike. Another major target among the textile strikers was the *tienda de raya* and its abuses. After the owner of one such store fired on workers in Río Blanco, Veracruz, it was burned to the ground, along with many others in the area (the struggle came to be known, for this reason, as the Río Blanco strike).

Both strikes were finally brought to an end through the use of repression. In Río Blanco and its environs between fifty and seventy workers were killed in attacks on crowds, armed skirmishes, and subsequent summary executions. In the case of Cananea, the Díaz regime allowed the company, which was US owned, to invite US Army Rangers over the border to help carry out the repression (after quickly swearing them in as Sonoran state militiamen). The ensuing outcry helped greatly erode the credibility of the Díaz dictatorship, and severely tarnished the claim that he could peacefully lead the country to progress.

Workers in Mexico were thus increasingly participating in the conflicts and campaigns associated with mass union organization. By 1910, with the launch of Madero's presidential campaign against Díaz, many artisans and industrial workers eagerly took up the young reformer's banner. Industrial workers hoped that the democratic opening Madero promised would provide them with increased opportunities to organize, as well as some measure of protective legislation in the workplace. Later on, as we'll see, Mexican workers and their unions would be an important wild card in the armed conflicts that erupted between the different revolutionary camps.

The Revolution: Many Different Pieces in Motion

As should be clear, a variety of social groups and motivations were in play over the course of the Revolution. Moreover, in terms of leaders, few revolutions have had as diverse and contradictory a cast of characters as Mexico did from 1910 to 1920. As mentioned previously, the Revolution's leaders all fought against one another, and none of them met a peaceful end. There was a great deal of conflict—including armed conflict—among the various camps within the Revolution itself, following the fall of Porfirio Díaz. Thus Zapata gave his support to Madero's rebellion, but then continued the armed agrarian struggle against his government; Pancho Villa was allied with, then broke with, then bloodily fought Carranza and his general Obregón; Carranza claimed to support land reform, but his forces attempted to crush Zapata's movement, and eventually orchestrated his assassination; and Obregón finally assumed power by rebelling against his former chief, Carranza, who was killed as he fled the revolt.

The details of this story, and their significance, will be discussed in the pages to follow. But it can all seem very confusing at first. Some have responded to the history of shifting conflicts, loyalties, and even political programs of the various camps by arguing that the Revolution can only be understood as a process driven by personal rivalries and ambitions, and their associated opportunistic struggles for power. From this standpoint, then, there is little to be learned by looking at the Revolution in terms of political and social conflict. To paraphrase Shakespeare, it was a tale full of sound and fury, but ultimately signified nothing. This sort of approach, however, is insufficient as a means to understanding the shifting course of events between 1910 and 1920.

A key point to understand concerning the Mexican Revolution is that it did not consist of a single movement. It was not led by a single political party, nor did it mobilize only one social class. Indeed, of the major camps within the Revolution, only that of Zapata and his allies, based in the campesinos of the "free" villages, was highly homogeneous in class terms. The Revolution is thus best understood by looking at the various social forces it unleashed—from campesinos to middle-class reformers to industrial workers to disgruntled landlords—and the goals and aspirations they developed. The different revolutionary camps and leaders did not simply float unattached above these various sorts of people and their visions of what the Revolution should accomplish. It was from this source—the long-standing discontent of different social groups, now openly expressed—that the Revolution's camps formed political programs and leaders formed worldviews.

Yet the worldview of the educated middle-class reformer, for example, and the rebel campesino were often very different. While many revolutionaries adhered to a political and social vision associated with middle-class aspirations, to prevail they also had to appeal to social forces—like campesinos or workers—that held different ones. This was especially the case as the Revolution unfolded over time, and agrarian radicalism and labor organizing could not be ignored even by those leaders (like the conservative landowner Carranza) who wanted to have nothing to do with either. Thus as the Revolution progressed, the various camps united, broke apart, and came into conflict as these different political visions or goals for the Revolution were laid bare.

So how did these various conflicts ultimately play out? It is to this question that we now turn. The answer begins with the efforts of Mexico's most earnest democrat, the wealthy young idealist Francisco Madero. He challenged the mighty Porfirio Díaz for the presidency, and—to nearly everyone's surprise—he succeeded, although it required armed revolt. As the defeated Díaz left Mexico to go into exile, he issued a prophetic statement: "Madero has unleashed a tiger—we will see if he can tame it." The Revolution was under way.

2

1910–1914

As laid out in section 1, the Mexican Revolution's root causes involved a combination of extremely rapid capitalist economic transformation in the countryside and a closed and dictatorial political system. The former led to mass dispossession of the lands and traditional rights of Mexico's rural villages, due to the huge profits to be made in commercial and export agriculture. The latter severely restricted the prospects for political and economic advancement of Mexico's middle classes, who became increasingly embittered with the regime. These two combined factors produced widespread revolt across Mexico after 1910. The story begins with the efforts of Francisco Madero, who attempted something not done before: to seriously challenge the dictator Porfirio Díaz in a presidential election.

The Spark: Madero's Presidential Campaign

To his contemporaries, Madero would have seemed like an unlikely anti-Porfirian dissident, and an even less likely armed rebel, national president, or revolutionary martyr. He came from one of Mexico's wealthiest landlord-capitalist families, one with numerous connections to the old regime. Indeed, one of Madero's long-standing friends was José Limantour, Porfirio Díaz's minister of finance. Yet Madero was also a highly unconventional man for his time and his country. He was educated abroad, in France and California; he was a Spiritist, and had held séances to communicate with the dead; he was

a strict vegetarian and a believer in homeopathic medicine, and did not drink alcohol; he provided schooling and health care for the workers and tenants on his properties; and he had even once been seen crying in public, at a funeral for a friend. Madero certainly didn't fit the later profile of the Mexican revolutionary, wearing a

Francisco Madero

cartridge belt and sombrero: he was a short, slender man, often appearing in public wearing a stuffy-looking bowler hat and dark suit.

Also unconventional was the fact that in a time and place in which a profound cynicism about politics reigned, Madero remained a passionate believer in the virtues of Liberal democracy. In Mexico, this meant free and fair elections rather than stolen ones; constitutional government rather than arbitrary rule; inalienable individual rights over the many abuses by

Madero arriving at a campaign rally

state; and the rule of law over corruption. During his presidential campaign he would declare that "liberty, by itself, will resolve all problems. . . . Once the people can elect their representatives to Congress, the legitimate representatives will enact all the laws necessary for the growth and prosperity of the Republic."[1] Madero was clearly more of a political reformer—perhaps even a utopian one—than a social radical, but no one could doubt his sincerity.

So how did such an oddball best the mighty Díaz? Mexico's rulers would have never foreseen it. Madero's own grandfather, upon hearing of his plans to challenge Díaz in the presidential elections, referred to it as "a microbe's challenge to an elephant."[2] The possibility of wider revolt seemed even less likely. In 1909 the influential newspaper *El Imparcial* announced that "a revolution in Mexico is impossible." This view was echoed by the US industrialist Andrew Carnegie, who after a visit to Mexico in 1910 declared that "in all of the corners of the Republic an enviable peace reigns."[3] They were mistaken of course, and ironically it was Díaz himself who first cracked open the Pandora's box of revolt.

The aging dictator, knowing he had only a few years left, had become increasingly concerned with his international image and his place in history. Perhaps given his increasing penchant for repression, he didn't wish to be seen, in the last instance, as a thug, especially after all he believed he had done for Mexico. So in 1908, in an interview with US journalist James Creelman for *Pearson's Magazine*, Díaz announced his willingness to accept a political opposition, and even an opposition presidential candidate, in Mexico. His later behavior showed him to be utterly insincere, but the resulting fawning article—titled "President Díaz: Hero of the Americas"—caused a stir across the country. The regime's own supporters, and those who carried out its repression, were unsure how to proceed. This provided a space for democrats like Madero to assert themselves.

It's not that Mexico didn't have local and national elections under Díaz. But they were largely for show, fixed according to what contemporaries called "the usual methods"—ballot stuffing, vote buying, and, if necessary, physical intimidation. The winning candidate for a governorship or a congressional seat was typically settled in advance via horse-trading among the wealthy. And at the presidential level, the winning candidate was always Porfirio Díaz. But the Creelman interview set off a wave of speculation and negotiation among middle-class political reformers and anxious members of the landowning and business elite.

The latter were mainly worried about ensuring a stable political succession; Díaz was almost eighty years old, and an heir had to be found. In addition, some members of the economic elite were dissatisfied with the regime and hoped for change. Democracy was not the issue here. Díaz's technocratic advisers, the highly unpopular científicos, were regarded as increasingly managing the economy, and government fiscal policy, in the interest of foreign bankers. Foreign investors were also seen as enjoying a few too many privileges in the later years of the regime. This concern was especially common among capitalists in the booming states of the Mexican north, who, while they depended on access to US markets, did not like to see the gringos heading south and throwing their weight around. Francisco Madero's family was among these. The deep recession of 1908, a consequence of Mexico's increasing integration into the global economic system, further exacerbated such frustrations.

A loose coalition of wealthy and middle-class reformers finally settled on a potential successor: Bernardo Reyes, a popular military general and governor of the northern state of Nuevo León. Reyes had always been a loyal member of the system, but was also viewed as not beholden to the hated científicos. A campaign began, not to challenge Díaz, but merely to make Reyes his vice-presidential candidate, in opposition to Díaz's nomination of a científico crony. President Díaz, however, feeling threatened, put the kibosh on this succession plan. Even the timid pro-Reyes political campaign was more than the dictator could countenance, despite his fine words in the Creelman interview. Reyes was ordered on a diplomatic mission to Europe—to undertake a study of military tactics, it was said—an assignment he meekly accepted. The científico was kept as vice-presidential candidate, and those who had sought cautious, incremental change were left empty-handed.

Into this gap stepped Francisco Madero, who was running a presidential campaign directly against Díaz, under the banner of his Anti-Reelectionist Party. His slogan was a simple one: *sufragio efectivo y no reelección*—effective suffrage and no reelection. Far more than the Reyes campaign, his program was a principled appeal to those who saw Liberal democracy as a path to further national progress and a restraint on the rampant political privilege and corruption throughout government. And unlike Reyes, he was willing to politically challenge the regime. The long-suffering Liberal middle-class opposition in Mexico increasingly flocked to his banner.

Madero also obtained a great deal of urban working-class support. He advocated freedom of association—derived from Mexico's long-ignored Constitution of 1857—which meant that workers should have the right to organize themselves as anyone else might. This would allow them to form "strong associations, so that, united, you will be able to defend your own rights," as Madero told a rally of textile workers.[4] For Madero this did not mean government intervention to regulate wages and working conditions, or legalized collective bargaining. But his message gave urban workers some hope in an increased freedom to organize, and they rewarded Madero with widespread backing. By the summer of 1910 there were some thirty working-class Maderista clubs across Mexico.[5]

This political opening did not last long, however. Díaz soon realized that Madero might actually win the election if he was allowed to continue, in spite of the regime's "usual methods." After a speech in the northern city of San Luis Potosí, the young scion was arrested for "attempts at rebellion and insults to the authorities," and was thrown behind bars. Not long after, Díaz was smoothly, and dubiously, "elected" for the eighth time. Soon the lavish celebrations of the centennial of Mexican independence began in the capital. Díaz and his regime seemed to have prevailed yet again.

The Unexpected Blaze

At this stage, sitting in prison, his electoral campaign in tatters, Madero appears to have finally decided that armed revolt would be the only way to dislodge the dictator and bring democracy to Mexico. His friends within the regime soon helped to get him out of his cell and placed under house arrest. Disguising himself as a laborer, Madero then fled the country and issued his famous "Plan de San Luis Potosí" from San Antonio, Texas. It repeated Madero's political denunciations of the regime, while declaring the recent elections to be null and void and Madero to be the provisional president of Mexico. It was a cautious document, largely avoiding social questions, while affirming that Madero sought "to avoid as far as possible the disorders inevitable in any revolutionary movement." Perhaps revealing his own inexperience in these matters, Madero declared that the rebellion in support of his plan was to begin at 6:00 p.m. sharp on November 20, 1910.

When the time came, Madero's revolt appeared to be a complete disaster at first. The police and army were obviously forewarned. His various urban middle-class conspirators were quickly arrested, when not killed. For his part, Madero elected to remain in Texas. But this was not to be the end of the story.

Significantly, in the Plan de San Luis Madero had also appealed, in a limited way, to the nation's campesino population. The plan noted that the cases of those who had been "deprived of their lands" under the dictatorship would be "subject to review" by the government. Moreover, those who had lost lands through "immoral means" would have them returned, by force of law. As with the working class, Madero attempted to tread a fine line between reaching out to plebeian supporters and making promises he did not wish to keep. But it didn't matter: even lip service to their hopes and demands was something campesinos had not heard from a major political figure in decades. Most already believed they had lost their lands by "immoral means." Madero, moreover, was calling on them to pick up a gun. In response, Mexico's campesinos would act in a way that Madero's other sympathizers had not: they would take up arms on a massive scale. It was this ongoing agrarian mobilization over the next ten years—at times rising, at times falling, but never fully crushed—that made the Revolution such a bitter and polarized conflict.

Madero's call for revolt initially found the greatest resonance in the northern state of Chihuahua and its environs. Due to its dependence on mineral and beef exports, this state had been hit harder than others in the 1908 recession. Moreover, it was ruled by a particularly corrupt and dictatorial family clan, at the top of which stood Luis Terrazas, easily Mexico's largest landowner. Resentment of the Porfirian system ran deep, and conditions were ripe for revolt.

Chihuahua was also home to José Doroteo Arango, a man in his early thirties who had held various legal and illegal occupations over the course of his life, from cattle rustler to muleteer to armed bandit. It was said he first ran afoul of the law in his home state of Durango, when as a young man he shot a local hacienda administrator who had tried to rape his sister. Whatever the truth of the matter was, when Madero called for revolt he was on the run from the authorities once again. The Chihuahuan revolutionaries quickly recruited him: after all, he had no love for the Porfirian authorities, he knew the countryside well, and he was known to be an excellent horseman and a crack shot with both pistol and rifle. Arango recruited a small band of his fellow outlaws and scored the first rebel victory in Chihuahua in a minor skirmish with federal troops. His audacity soon became legendary: at one point he attacked an army column of seven hundred soldiers with only ten men on horseback. This unlikely rebel would go down in history as the infamous Pancho Villa.

It was the varied Chihuahuan irregular forces like Villa's that largely broke the back of Díaz's rule. They were described by one contemporary critic as "rogues or killers escaped from justice, ignorant ranchers, coarse muleteers, bankrupt crackpots, [and] failed students and professionals." Another noted that many of their leaders had "more or less open accounts with the government for crimes unpunished."[6] There will be more to say on the composition of the Chihuahuan forces later, but these assessments (leaving aside their deprecatory character) were not that far from the truth. Along with ranchers, bandits, and "coarse muleteers," there were migrant workers, unemployed miners, ranch hands, and cowboys. The troops also included residents of the northern military colonies—communities that had been given land and weapons in past decades to fight the Apaches. These were people who strongly valued a readiness to fight, and the ability to ride a horse and use a rifle. Taken together, this was the nucleus of what would later become Villa's Northern Division, the most impressive fighting force Mexico had ever seen. They were local people who knew the terrain in which they operated, and they made for ready and hardened fighters—men who could ride all night on horseback on empty stomachs and mount a merciless surprise attack at dawn. As they increasingly came together, Díaz's Federal Army did not stand a chance.

But Madero's revolt was not limited to the Mexican north. A year before the stolen presidential election, an equally momentous election took place, although no one would have known it at the time. It was for leadership of the village of Anenecuilco in the state of Morelos—not far from the great capital Mexico City, but in many respects a world away. The village was seven centuries old, and some of its ancient title deeds had been written in the Nahuatl language of the Aztecs. On September 12, 1909, a respected local

Pancho Villa

horse trainer and small rancher was elected municipal president. His family had a long and proud history of fighting in Mexico's nineteenth-century patriotic wars. The rest of the new village leadership were young men like himself, all determined to fight the growing abuses perpetrated by the local sugar haciendas. His name was Emiliano Zapata.

Zapata already had a reputation among the local authorities as a troublemaker, and that would only increase in his new role. The following year he began organizing the repossession of hacienda lands in Morelos, with armed campesinos tearing down boundary fences and distributing plots among local villagers. His notoriety and popularity grew across the state, and Zapata was soon on the run from the law, albeit with a growing group of followers. Many of his supporters were poorly armed, and fought in the same clothes they wore to harvest their corn. Nonetheless, a motivated campesino wielding a country machete could be a formidable fighter. Soon Zapata's rebel forces began to equip themselves by stealing weapons and horses from local landlords; in one case they hijacked a train and drove the locomotive straight through the hacienda gates. In March 1911 Zapata and his troops formally joined Madero's revolt, taking on the army in the areas south of the capital.

Ultimately it was Madero's campesino supporters, fighting on various fronts, who made the difference. On May 9, Villa was among the rebels who took the strategic border city of Ciudad Juárez. On May 15, rebels took the key northern railroad hub of Torreón after the Federal Army fled. On May 19, Zapata, commanding some four thousand men, captured the city of Cuautla in Morelos—roughly twenty miles from the outskirts of Mexico City—after heavy fighting. Soon after, federal troops surrendered

Emiliano Zapata (center) and his officers

Cuernavaca, the state capital. The writing was on the wall. On May 25, 1911, the once-invincible Porfirio Díaz resigned and handed over the presidency to a caretaker. He boarded the ship *Ypiranga* the following day, en route to exile in Europe. On October 1 of that same year, Madero was overwhelmingly elected president of Mexico. Díaz, for his part, never returned to his native country: he died in exile in 1915 and was buried in Paris.

The Zapatista Tiger Is Loose

The old Porfirian elite might have come to forgive Madero for pushing Díaz into the dustbin of history. But there was always a problem with him in their eyes: Madero was too sincere in his democratic and constitutional ideals. When it came time to use a firm hand against rural revolt in Mexico, try as he might, nothing the new president would do was good enough for them. Although Madero was far from being a radical, and certainly not tolerant of campesino rebellion, this little man in the bowler hat, this vegetarian oddball who prattled on about political liberty and fair elections—for the rich, he could not be trusted. Indeed, it's fair to say that many of them despised him. They were nostalgic for the old General Díaz, who had proved time and again that he would mercilessly defend their interests against the rabble. Instead, all of Madero's democratic reforms were just making the poor more insolent and unmanageable. To his misfortune, Madero was—to paraphrase one of his supporters—a thoroughly bourgeois reformer whom the bourgeoisie simply refused to support.

From their perspective, Madero's campaign had "unleashed a tiger," to use Porfirio Díaz's phrase; the old dictator had further added: "Let us see if he [Madero] can control it." Ultimately, Madero could not. The contemporary intellectual Luis Cabrera noted that almost immediately "the great country estate saw itself threatened on all sides."[7] Madero's victory unleashed an explosion of agrarian radicalism—and campesino revenge—across much of the country. The Zapatista movement was only the best-organized and most visible example of this. Indeed, Cabrera warned Madero in a letter that he was "confronted with an upheaval more powerful and more vast than what you had in mind." The only solution was to "stamp it out."[8] This was easier said than done, however: as a result of Madero's original call to revolt, there were now some sixty thousand men under arms across the country. And in many cases their guns started to be turned on hated politicians and landlords.[9]

Well before Madero's election, armed villagers led by Zapata

Anti-Díaz rebels with a makeshift cannon

had begun occupying the lands of the sugar plantations in Morelos, while their powerless owners and administrators, according to historian John Womack, "had no alternative but to meet the revolutionary demands." In the Laguna, the rich agricultural region to the north, one contemporary observer noted that sharecroppers and renters had begun to seize hacienda land, since in their view, "as the Maderistas have won, they have the right to take [it] and are, in fact, owners of the land."[10] In nearby Torreón, meanwhile, the plebeians of the city, according to one horrified report, were "displaying an improper equality . . . [and] obliging ladies and respectable people to walk in the middle of the streets," rather than on the sidewalk. The streets at this time of year, the rainy season, were filled with mud.

Elsewhere, in the village of Iguapalapa in the state of Guerrero, the indigenous residents armed themselves, occupied the agricultural land and pasture they had lost, and retook their land titles by armed force. Those who resisted, including the local priest, were shot. At the Catmis hacienda in the Yucatán, the landlords, two brothers with cruel reputations, "were killed by the weapons of their own servants." In Temax, in the same state, the jefe político was taken to the town square by angry villagers, tied to a chair, and "riddled with bullets." The fifty haciendas in the Apam region of Hidalgo were, in the words of one military officer, "constantly requesting protection for their persons and property." According to another report, in the state of Michoacán "armed Indians [were] organizing for the purpose of dispossessing landlords, . . . [claiming] lands belonging to their ancestors, because 'Madero said we could have them.'" At the hacienda Sierra Prieta, not far from the capital, the peones complained to the landlord about their low wages. His response was to cut them further. As a result, a group of forty peones attempted to meet with the administrator of the estate; he refused to see them and ordered them punished. Enraged, they forced their way into his office. His body was later found with forty stab wounds, one for each peón.[11]

Stories like these poured in from all over the country, alarming not only the landlords but the new president as well. For Madero had wanted no such thing. He was a landlord and capitalist himself, a kindhearted one to be sure, but not one who advocated that the campesinos take matters into their own hands. His promise that land questions would be "subject to review" implied an orderly, legal process, rather than land seizure or revolt. Yet for campesinos such a process would mean turning to the lawyers and judges they already mistrusted, to obtain the land they already knew was their own.

And so Madero's campesino supporters, who were, in the words of historian Alan Knight, "expecting speedy redress," soon "experienced swift disillusionment."[12] Many were unwilling to wait for the political liberty Madero had promised would arrive, and moreover had little confidence that it would address their problems. It was not long before some of Madero's original allies would rise up against him, raising the banner of agrarian reform and accusing his government of failing to carry it out. The most intractable of these revolts was undoubtedly the Zapatista movement in Morelos.

In the months following the victory of the Madero rebellion, Zapata and his campesino followers would become increasingly frustrated and disappointed with their future president. Not long after Díaz's resignation, outside Madero loyalists had swept into Morelos and occupied a number of towns. One of Zapata's lieutenants was quickly executed for taxing the rich of the region. A new governor was appointed without consultation with Zapata: he was a former head of the Bank of Morelos and unquestionably pro-landlord. Although Zapata was clearly the principal authority in the state, a message was being sent. Moreover, the accords that had secured Díaz's departure required all revolutionary troops to disarm, while reestablishing the authority of the defeated Federal Army. It was a concession that rankled many of the rebels, including the Zapatistas. Historian John Womack characterizes the speed with which the landlords regained political control in Morelos as "astounding"—as it probably seemed to Zapata and his followers, who had not expected such reversals after Madero's victory.[13]

Prior to his formal election to the presidency, Madero met personally with Zapata in Morelos and tried to convince him to disarm his forces and accept Madero's promises that land questions would eventually be "subject to review." This meant, however, that the lands the campesinos had taken would have to be returned to the haciendas. Indeed, Madero was busy attempting to restore the *status quo ante*—at least between campesino and landlord—in as many areas of Mexico as possible. Of Zapata's roughly 4,000 men, Madero proposed that some 250 would be given jobs as rural policemen; the rest would have to turn in their weapons. Meanwhile the Federal Army, its authority restored, was menacingly encircling Morelos. Zapata's brother found Madero's approach so disingenuous—"this little man has already betrayed the cause"—that he wanted him lynched on the spot.[14]

But the reality was that the Zapatistas' and Madero's causes were never the same. Carrying out widespread agrarian reform was certainly not on Madero's agenda. His main concern was implementing reforms at the level of formal politics, which he believed would improve the lot of all Mexicans. He thus argued that "the people do not want bread, but liberty." Change would come through the ballot box—"a new weapon which you have won"—rather than further rebellion. Or as he noted in a speech the following year, "It has been maintained that the object of the San Luis revolution was to resolve the agrarian problem; that is not correct. The revolution was to recover our liberty." If campesinos wanted land, they had to obtain it "by means of hard work." Indeed, it would be "utterly absurd to demand that the government should acquire the big properties and divide them among smallholders." Later Madero would denounce the "amorphous agrarian socialism" which he believed to be "peculiar to the simple minds of the peasants of Morelos" rebelling under Zapata.[15]

Indeed, Zapata's "peculiar" political approach mirrored the qualities of the campesinos he led: after decades of robbery and betrayal, they were a taciturn, suspicious, stubborn, intransigent people who did not take well to being sweet-talked. Madero at times seemed exasperated with popular leaders like Zapata, who would not give up their supporters' demands and await the maturation of his vision. The negotiations between Madero and the Zapatistas, not surprisingly, did not amount to much.

And so on November 28, 1911, the "Revolutionary Council of the State of Morelos" broke with the new president and issued the famous Plan de Ayala. It was signed by Zapata and the fifty-eight other members of the council, most of whom could barely write their names. Madero was denounced as a traitor to the very cause he had championed, because of his collaboration and compromises with the old Porfirian landed elite. At the center of the plan was the question of agrarian reform. All of the "land, woodlands and waters" taken by the landlords, it proclaimed, "shall become forthwith the property of villagers or citizens who have the appropriate deeds and have been dispossessed through the trickery of our oppressors." The document added that "such property will be resolutely defended with arms in hand." Moreover, "any

Zapatista recruitment poster

usurpers who claim the right to it must argue their case before special courts to be established at the victory of the revolution."

This was a crucial revolutionary measure. Note that now it was not the campesinos who had to go to court to prove they had a right to the land; it was in fact the landlords who would have to go to court to do so. It was an approach, as historian Adolfo Gilly has noted, that stood the established legality of property rights on its head.[16] In addition, in revolutionary Morelos even "the appropriate deeds" were not necessary: if the village elders remembered that the village's boundaries were so, then so it would be. The memory of the campesino had more weight than the documented property rights of the landlord.

Lastly, for good measure, the plan added, "Hacendados, científicos, and local bosses who directly or indirectly oppose this plan will have their property nationalized." In Morelos, this essentially meant all the large landlords in the state. It would certainly mean close to the same in the rest of the country. In short, the Plan de Ayala was a document that called for the radical transformation of rural property relations in Mexico and the reversal of established property rights laws, all to be carried out by armed action, and the maintenance of this transformation by postrevolutionary force of law. While they fought, the Zapatistas would directly put this program into practice in Morelos.

The Death of the Liberal Revolution

Given the depth of the conflict, Madero's policy with restive campesinos like the Zapatistas ultimately went beyond speeches and admonitions. His grandfather, the family patriarch, had given the young president stern advice to "repress any new movement which seeks to introduce disorder . . . [by] punishing its authors with the greatest severity."[17] Indeed, the idea of crushing agrarian revolt, and Zapata's movement in particular, was highly popular among the supporters of the old regime. Editorial cartoons in the Porfirian press of the capital often depicted Zapata as a barbarous savage, waving a bloodstained sword, juggling skulls, and even eating human flesh. The conservative newspaper *El Imparcial* further called for an "energetic purification" of Morelos, to put down "Zapata and his troglodyte hosts." The role of the village population, and its support for the guerrillas, was also clear:

> It comes to the notice of an army unit that a band of Zapatistas has appeared in the vicinity, committing, as is their wont, all manner of outrages. The army immediately sets out for the place in question. What will it find? It finds a peaceful village: young men with spades in their hands; women bent over their grinding-stones; the authorities trying to discover the whereabouts of the men who attacked nearby haciendas find sad expressions and frightened looks. Where are the Zapatistas? Where are the Zapatistas? . . . The Zapatistas have not moved, they are here, here they are! Rifles have turned into spades, cartridge-belts into spindles, a den into a garden, a bandit into a laborer. . . . If they have disappeared so completely, it is because they could merge with the crowd who creates and hides them, like steam dissolving into the very water from which it originated.[18]

President Madero soon began to appoint a series of merciless army generals to carry out scorched-earth campaigns against the villages in Morelos. The generals took to this mission with zeal, engaging in large-scale massacres, the burning of homes and fields, and expulsion of village populations. Their goal was to forcibly put down the Zapatistas and their supporters, and to protect the landlords and their property.

Moreover, the use of repression in response to rural revolt and protest was not limited to Morelos. To take a different case, from San Luis Potosí: there a group of sharecroppers had demanded an increase in the price their landlord paid for a bundle of grain, from sixty centavos to one peso. They threatened to sell their produce directly to local merchants if they were denied. The landlord refused to negotiate and contacted the local Maderista authorities. Troops arrived, and two of the sharecroppers' leaders were hanged on the spot. The remaining campesinos were arrested and taken to the state capital, where they were eventually released by the state governor.[19]

This willingness to use military force would come back to haunt Madero. One of the generals he assigned to put down the Zapatista rebellion was the infamous Victoriano Huerta, a Porfirio Díaz loyalist who had become the new president's point man in dealing with revolt. He would later be the man who would order Madero's murder.

Yet despite this eventual fate, throughout his brief presidency Madero did his best to actively court the old Porfirian elite, and particularly the Federal Army. By 1913, the year it overthrew him, the army was more powerful than it had ever been before. Madero spent more than twice what Díaz had spent on the military, using nearly one-third of the government budget for this purpose. Otherwise government expenditure and budget priorities changed little, if at all, from the Díaz era. The army's numbers increased from twenty thousand to seventy thousand men, and Madero personally wooed the generals and officers with expensive gifts and easy promotions.[20] In addition, the old Porfirian political class was largely kept in place throughout Madero's government, much to the consternation of his supporters.

Many of Madero's allies in fact pointedly warned him of the dangers of conciliating the representatives of the old regime and abandoning the popular forces that had brought him to power. A group of congressional supporters at one point appealed to the president in a letter, noting that "the revolution is heading towards collapse and pulling down the government to which it gave rise, for the simple reason that it has not ruled with revolutionaries. Compromises and concessions to the supporters of the old regime are the main causes of the unsettling situation in which the government . . . finds itself. . . . The regime appears relentlessly bent on suicide."[21] Another Maderista, writing from the restive Laguna region, noted that those who had fought for Madero "see no practical benefit from the struggle in which they helped you: the land is not divided; not even the smallest communities' property, which the big proprietors seized from them, has been restored; the worker is not supported in his demands."[22] In short, Madero was far from oblivious to the anger and frustration at the bottom of society. What he seems to have been oblivious to was the growing danger coming from the top.

Notwithstanding his lack of action on land distribution, and despite the ongoing bloodbath in Morelos, it would be unfair to say that Madero accomplished only repression during his rule. He was committed to his political reforms and achieved a number of them: elections in Mexico, although flawed, were freer than ever before, political parties were freer than ever before, the press was freer than ever before, and the national Congress was freer than ever before. But ironically, given the continued political and economic power of the Porfirian elite, these various institutions largely focused on attacking Madero himself. His enemies made it their goal to undermine—and eventually destroy—his presidency, with the army being the final *punta de lanza*, the spear point. Perhaps Madero's greatest weakness—in terms of his own survival, and that of his government—was his faith in the established rule of law, and his belief that the old Porfirian reactionaries also shared it. He was gravely mistaken, and it cost him his life.

Meanwhile, the US government was not standing by. It was deeply concerned with the ongoing conflicts in Mexico and the threats to the considerable assets of US investors in the country. President William Howard Taft clearly took notice; as he wrote to his secretary of state at the time, "I am getting to point where I think we ought to put a little dynamite for the purpose of stirring up that dreamer [Madero] who seems unfitted to meet the crisis in the country of which he is President."[23] The most active role, however, was surely that of US ambassador Henry Lane Wilson. For Mexicans, he has gone down in history as a villain. Wilson effectively promised anyone in Mexico who would listen that if they overthrew Madero they could count on US support. Indeed, the final accord between the anti-Madero conspirators was settled in the offices of the US Embassy and came to be known as the notorious "Embassy Pact."

Two key figures in the toppling of the Madero government were the aforementioned General Bernardo Reyes (the failed vice-presidential hopeful), and Felix Díaz, a military officer and nephew of the former dictator. They had each independently started a counterrevolutionary rebellion against Madero, both of which had ended in pathetic failure. Both men had been captured, and in each case Madero elected not to follow his grandfather's advice regarding those who "introduced disorder"—at least for those among the elite—and so Díaz and Reyes were given cushy jail terms that allowed them to freely meet with their supporters in Mexico City. Not surprisingly, they continued to conspire against the government. In early February 1913 the two men were freed from jail by sympathizers in the army, and declared themselves—once again—in revolt. After some initial skirmishes, the rebels barricaded themselves in a fortress in the capital, the Ciudadela. This was the beginning of the Decena Trágica—the tragic ten days that led to Madero's ouster.

The head of the army had been seriously wounded in the outbreak of the revolt, and Madero appointed General Victoriano Huerta to succeed him. Huerta, however, was soon was playing both sides, in part under the influence of US ambassador Wilson. He began secretly negotiating with the coup plotters about a post-Madero government. At the same time, Huerta was sending loyal troops on suicide missions against the rebels' well-defended positions in the Ciudadela. The shelling of the fortress also consistently seemed to miss the mark, although it killed plenty of people in the surrounding neighborhoods. Huerta was essentially holding out, playing hardball with the other plotters, hoping to emerge as top dog in the end.

Madero had one last chance to undermine the coming coup. His hard-nosed brother Gustavo rightly suspected that General Huerta was conspiring with the rebels rather than fighting them. Late one night, as the standoff continued in the capital, he brought the general to the president's offices—at gunpoint—and explained the suspected plot to his brother. Huerta vigorously professed his innocence. He was lying of course, but Madero believed him and gave him another chance to prove his loyalty. Gustavo was told to

Scene in front of Mexico's National Palace during the Decena Trágica

put away his weapon, to restrain himself, and Huerta was let go. The following day—February 18, 1913—the general returned to the National Palace at the head of rebel troops. He arrested President Madero, forced him to resign, and assumed the presidency. The young reformer had remained in power only fifteen months.

The Thug They Had Hoped For

The old Porfirian elite—from the landlords, to powerful businessmen and bankers, to the Church hierarchy, to the army brass—were thrilled at Huerta's accession. He was just the unreconstructed thug the old elite wanted in power to deal with the poor. There would thankfully be no more of Madero's attempts to reconcile their rule with constitutional niceties. Two days after the coup, General

Huerta and his new cabinet attended a lavish party at the US Embassy, where there were toasts to his future success. The archbishop of Mexico had a Te Deum sung at Mass in honor of the new president. Huerta soon after announced to Mexico's Congress—a body he would later dissolve—that he would "re-establish peace, cost what it may."[24]

General Huerta's seventeen-month dictatorial presidency was highly brutal, and at times also quite bizarre. He was a notorious drunkard, and held many of his cabinet meetings in various bars in the capital. On one occasion he had his entire cabinet arrested for not wearing the emblems and sashes required of generals in civilian clothing. Huerta was also reportedly an avid pot smoker; it is said that a variant of the old folk tune "La cucaracha" came to be sung in mockery of him:

> La cucaracha, la cucaracha
> Ya no puede caminar
> Porque le falta, porque no tiene
> Marihuana que fumar![25]

But it was Huerta's brutality that most stood out. As the German ambassador to Mexico, a Huerta supporter, noted, "the government displays a corruptibility and depravity that exceeds anything known in the past. . . . This terrorism is not that of an enlightened autocrat but is currently assuming the form of a senseless rage." Of his methods, the ambassador added, "We could look upon them with equanimity if they were not occasionally extended to foreigners."[26]

The first victims were Madero and his closest collaborators. His brother Gustavo had his one good eye gouged out, and was beaten and stabbed to death by Huerta's soldiers. Abraham

General Victoriano Huerta (center) and his cabinet

González, a moderate reformer and the Maderista governor of Chihuahua, was thrown under a moving train. And Madero himself was summarily executed, along with his vice president, while being transferred to a federal penitentiary. He was allegedly "attempting to escape," a fiction few tried to maintain. Before long prominent critics of the government were being "disappeared" or forced to flee the country, after the army robbed them of any wealth they had. Most of the country's state governors were soon replaced by military men, and later that year, in October 1913, Congress was formally dissolved. Another dictator was in charge, although one more crass and cruel than Díaz had ever been.

While in detention awaiting his fate, José María Pino Suárez, Madero's vice president, had written to a friend asking: "Will they have the stupidity to kill us? . . . They would gain nothing, for we would be greater in death than we are today in life."[27] Alas, they were indeed that stupid, and brutal. And it is also true that Madero became greater, as a symbol, in death than in life. For all the disillusionment with him, Madero's murder was met with widespread anguish and rage. His supporters, and his critics, vowed to avenge his death. Armed rebellion soon reappeared across Mexico.

The Rise of Carranza and the Constitutionalists

The original states in the anti-Huerta revolt—aside from Zapatista Morelos, where the rebels had never laid down their arms—were Chihuahua, Coahuila, and Sonora, running in a row across the northern border of Mexico. In general, the north was more prosperous, more literate, more commercially minded, and more middle-class than the rest of the country; it was the boom region of the Porfirian era. It might be an exaggeration to say that members of the new Maderista generation in this part of the country mainly wanted to be left alone, away from Porfirian corruption and control, so that they could make money. But exaggeration or not, this represented a key element of the opposition to Huerta in the north. Much of the rank and file, however, were still the ranch hands, muleteers, former miners, and military colonists who had followed men like Villa before, and would do so again. Fortunately, the previous Maderista rebel forces had maintained their weapons and organization in the north in form of state militias; the attempts by Madero to disarm them, or subsume them to the Federal Army's authority, had largely been resisted.

The key leader in this new phase was Venustiano Carranza, a prominent landowner and the governor of the state of Coahuila.

He and the governor of Sonora were the only ones not to recognize the new regime (the governor of Chihuahua, of course, was already dead). Carranza quickly gathered up the pro-Madero forces in the north; they named themselves the Constitutionalists, in reference to the Constitution of 1857, which had been violated with the military coup. A new national plan was unveiled, this one titled the Plan de Guadalupe.

This declaration, however, was far more conservative than Madero's original 1910 program for rebellion. The Plan de Guadalupe was extremely brief and pragmatic, and it included no mention whatsoever of social issues—merely an emphasis on the need to restore constitutional order to Mexico. There was none of Madero's talk of the great virtues of liberty and democracy.

Venustiano Carranza

Land reform was certainly not on the table. The plan further announced that "when the Constitutionalist Army occupies Mexico City, the citizen Venustiano Carranza, First Chief of the Army, will be in interim charge of the Executive Power." Carranza had a clear desire to centralize political power in his hands, and he jealously guarded his leadership role in the movement from the start.

But there was a sense, albeit a limited one, in which Carranza was more radical than Madero. Although his shadow cabinet was entirely made up of educated men wearing "waistcoats and neckties," they recognized from Madero's tragic experience that the old Porfirian political class and the army couldn't be conciliated.[28] They had to be crushed by force. Madero had been far too forgiving, tolerant, and naive, the Constitutionalist leaders believed, and he had been killed as a result. Indeed, if the new leaders had not rebelled, they might have all been killed as well, Carranza included. And so political niceties were now a thing of the past: the gloves had to come off. Many of these leaders were also highly suspicious of—if not hostile toward—the Catholic Church and the United States. This was in part due to the role that both played during the Huerta regime, and in part due to the perception that both would be obstacles to Mexico's future national development and progress.

The "First Chief" Carranza was ostensibly in command of the Constitutionalist armies. However, his relative conservatism—particularly on the issue of land reform—meant that he was never an unquestioned leader. Zapata in the south refused to recognize Carranza's command until he endorsed the Plan de Ayala, something Carranza would never do, given his pro-landlord views. Carranza also butted heads with the many radicals in his own ranks; this was especially true of his younger military officers, who were eager to bring about more profound changes in Mexico than those Carranza envisioned.

The most widely known of these officers was Pancho Villa, a leader in his own right, who consistently sought to maintain his independence from the First Chief. Carranza, however, desperately needed Villa—his military leadership and growing popularity were too valuable to ignore. He was thus made commander of the Northern Division, one of the Constitutionalist armies. Villa soon became the key military leader of the anti-Huerta phase of the Revolution, and it was largely thanks to the effectiveness of his forces that the Constitutionalists prevailed in spite of their differences. Along the way Villa also became a folk hero to the people of the Mexican north and beyond.

Pancho Villa: From Bandit to Hero

In the months leading up to Huerta's coup, Villa's future prominence would have seemed unlikely. He was at this point sitting in a cell in the Tlatelolco prison in Mexico City. How this came about is yet another episode in Villa's eventful life. Villa had remained a loyal Maderista throughout the reformer's short-lived presidency, serving as a respected commander in the Chihuahuan state militia. Yet General Huerta had quickly come to see Villa as a potential future rival or threat. In June 1912, he had Villa arrested on trumped-up charges of insubordination and stealing a horse. Huerta tried to have Villa executed on the spot for the crime; his back was literally up against the wall, with the executioners readying their rifles, before he was saved by the last-minute intervention of President Madero himself. Villa was then transferred to Mexico City to await trial. At this point Madero refused to intervene any further, out of fear of antagonizing Huerta.

Villa rightly feared for his life, and so he planned an escape, with the help of a young prison clerk he had befriended. Villa painstakingly filed the bars to the window of his cell over the course of weeks, concealing his handiwork with grease. A local band playing music outside the prison walls helped cover up the sounds of his labors. Villa finally walked out of the prison yard on Christmas Day, wearing the garb of an attorney and blowing his nose into a handkerchief. Villa's conspirators brought a car for him, despite his initial insistence that they flee the city on horseback. It was only six weeks before Huerta's coup; had Villa remained in prison much longer he would have surely been assassinated.

From there Villa fled to the United States, and in March 1913 he crossed back into Mexico, this time on horseback, ready to join the emerging struggle against Huerta. With him were eight men—including the young prison clerk—along with two pounds of sugar, two pounds of coffee, a pound of salt, and five hundred bullets per person. His first act was to attack one of Luis Terrazas' largest estates and summarily execute the administrator. The latter was a man despised by the local peones for numerous abuses, including reserving the privilege of sleeping with brides on their wedding night. Villa's various acts of popular retribution would become legendary: in another village he forced the local priest, who had refused to recognize a child he had fathered, to publicly confess to his sins in the village square. Villa subsequently tracked down Terrazas' eldest son and persuaded him to reveal the location of the family treasure. Soon after he would amass and lead the seemingly unstoppable forces of the Northern Division. Pancho Villa was back, and more admired (by the poor) and feared (by the rich) than ever before.

So how did Villa—who spent many years as a rural bandit before the outbreak of revolution—achieve this degree of popular support? His acts of "frontier justice" against hated authority figures were certainly well received among the poor. More generally,

Villa (fourth from left) and his officers

Soldiers of the Northern Division

according to historian Friedrich Katz, Villa was "a complex mixture of [twentieth-century] social revolutionary and nineteenth-century *caudillo*."[29] What does this mean? On the one hand, Villa carried out a range of social measures in Chihuahua that were quite radical for his day. He effectively nationalized wide swaths of territory previously owned by the state's hacendados, as well as a number of factories owned by Huerta supporters. Some of these properties were then administered by his generals to fund the Northern Division, but most passed directly into the hands of the state government. These measures were significant: Chihuahua, having experienced near-constant warfare and economic crisis, was facing a desperate food supply situation. In cities and towns under Villista control, the Northern Division distributed generous food rations to the urban poor, the unemployed, widows, and orphans. The price of beef was radically reduced by government decree. This was made possible in part by the seizure of the vast cattle herds of Luis Terrazas, whose cows were led to slaughterhouses to feed the region's poor and purchase arms for the Northern Division.

In general, Villa was more pragmatic than ideological in his politics. This meant that he was willing to carry out even highly radical measures when he thought they were necessary for victory. Zapata, meanwhile, had also come to be recognized for his revolutionary political program, the agrarian Plan de Ayala. Their commonalities undoubtedly drew the two men together during the course of the Revolution. However, there were also some key differences between Zapata's and Villa's forces. Whereas Zapata's movement in Morelos ultimately rested upon the local organization of collective-landowning villages, in Chihuahua (and northern Mexico as a whole) such tight-knit, relatively homogeneous social organization was far less common. People were much more mobile and relatively independent. Villa's army thus did not have the cohesive grassroots social base of the Zapatistas.

Villa therefore maintained his authority and commanded his army via the methods of the *caudillo*, the nineteenth-century military strongman. The caudillo, broadly speaking, could be characterized as having great personal charisma, courage in battle, skills with both horse and rifle, loyalty to those loyal to him, generosity with subordinates and the less fortunate, and a propensity for the quick and merciless use of violence. Villa had all these qualities in spades. In short, he took care of "his people," and they took care of him and obeyed his command. He was a man who would literally give a shivering soldier the shirt off his back; but should that soldier should ever desert, the punishment would be swift and probably lethal. In summary, Villa had acquired a powerful authority among his troops, and the population at large; some of it was due to the popular and often radical social measures he introduced, but some of it also stemmed from his highly effective caudillo-style leadership.

There is another important factor to mention regarding the composition of Villa's forces and how they cohered. The Northern Division, along with other armies, was also held together by the work of countless women. Known as *soldaderas* or Adelitas, they were responsible for provisioning many of the large forces that were quickly assembled during the Revolution, as well as cleaning weapons, washing uniforms, caring for the wounded, and burying the dead. They numbered as much as a third of the male combat troops, and moved when the armies moved, taking charge of the bedding, clothing, cookware, and provisions ranging from cornmeal to chiles to chickens. There were also some women who played a role as fighters; most disguised themselves as men to join in combat, but in certain cases women were able to fight openly.

The soldaderas are often referred to as "camp followers" in English, but they were more than followers: no large rebel army could function without them. As the writer Elena Poniatowska has noted, "Without the soldaderas, there is no Mexican Revolution." Some were the wives, lovers, sisters, or cousins of individual soldiers, whereas others worked for money. A woman might also sign on as the troops passed through her town or village, to escape the life she led in her hometown; at times soldaderas were also forcibly recruited, that is, kidnapped from their families. Many a revolutionary commander undoubtedly found a bride this way, via an ultimatum to her parents: give me her hand in marriage or *me la llevo*—I will take her with me. Poniatowska adds that in the various armies, often "the horses received better treatment than the women."[30]

Villa's army thus quickly gathered strength, and along with this, widespread fear and respect. Meanwhile, in the face of renewed rebellion, the Federal Army was far from respected, and less and less feared as time went on. Although its forces were larger and better equipped than ever before—due to the previous efforts of Madero—the army was also more incompetent and mismanaged than ever before. Corruption was rampant: officers routinely stole money and supplies, when they weren't stealing from and extorting the general population. Indeed, Huerta at one point told a foreign diplomat that "if I forbid the army to steal, it will revolt against me."[31] Its rank-and-file troops were the same unmotivated forced recruits employed under Díaz, and mass desertions became increasingly common. The army's desperation reached such a point that to prevent attacks on military trains, family members of leading revolutionaries were often taken hostage and forced to ride on board. Yet the army couldn't prevent Villa's Northern Division from besting it repeatedly in battle on the plains of the Mexican north and routing federal soldiers from cities and towns.

In certain cases it was Villa's unconventional tactics that made the difference. One example was the rebel victory at Chihuahua City, the capital of the state. After a frontal attack had failed, Villa's troops commandeered a military coal train some miles from town. The station's telegrapher was ordered to inform army headquarters that the train had to return to Chihuahua City because the rail lines had been cut by the enemy. Some two thousand armed Villistas then boarded the train, and at each station the local telegrapher was instructed—a gun to his head—to inform the authorities that all was well. Late at night they entered the city without resistance. The "Trojan train" trick worked—the Federals were caught completely by surprise, and the town fell to the rebels.

Villa also succeeded through the use of fear: the Federal Army leadership was given absolutely no quarter. His men, many of them military colonists accustomed to frontier warfare, expected no less from their enemies. Captured army officers were executed en masse. Madero's death was to be avenged. Some were shot stacked in groups of three or more to save on ammunition. As a result, many army leaders chose to abandon their posts and flee rather than face defeat and certain death at Villa's hands.

Villa's successes on the battlefield also got Washington's attention. The new Woodrow Wilson administration had soured on Huerta and his erratic and unstable rule, and was fishing around for a new strongman—someone, anyone, who could bring some measure of "order" to Mexico. President Wilson seems to have been taken by Villa's leadership abilities and personal authority. According to one diplomat, Wilson felt that Villa "represents the only instrument of civilization in Mexico. His firm authority allows him to create order and educate the turbulent mass of peons so prone to pillage."[32] Villa was believed to be a social radical of some undefined sort, but he had also been careful to leave US property alone, to avoid antagonizing the Americans while he fought Huerta. This was a different approach from that of the "First Chief" Carranza, who refused to make any concessions to the United States and often extracted military taxes from American businesspeople.

In the end, Wilson finally decided to act, rather than risk being completely sidelined by events. In February 1914, with half the country already in Constitutionalist hands, he lifted the US arms embargo on Mexico. This allowed weapons, which previously had had to be smuggled, to flow more easily over the northern border. Villa, meanwhile, seemed to enjoy the favorable attention from the north. He even allowed a film crew—from the Mutual Film Company—to come south of the border to record his battles, in order to make a movie starring Villa as himself. The movie has since been lost (some of the footage survives), but Villa received a twenty-five-thousand-dollar advance. His star was clearly on the rise.

President Wilson for his part continued to be very keen on moving events along in Mexico. His administration finally decided that a partial military occupation of the country would be necessary. Wilson had secretly proposed such a plan to Carranza and been immediately turned down, but this didn't really deter him. Wilson settled on the idea of directly occupying the port city of

Veracruz. Although Huerta's regime was clearly on the ropes, Wilson felt that by controlling the nation's principal port the United States could influence the national settlement after Huerta fell. In this he proved to be quite mistaken.

To invade another country a pretext had to be found, of course, and it was almost too silly to be believed: on April 9, 1914, a few US sailors were briefly detained in the gulf port of Tampico. They were released within two hours, with an official apology besides, but the US Navy admiral in charge issued an ultimatum. He demanded, as a penance of sorts, that the American flag be raised over the port and given a twenty-one-gun salute by Mexican troops. This was obviously a nonstarter. President Huerta proposed

US troops march in Veracruz

a salute to both flags, which was refused. In the meantime, President Wilson, with evidence of Mexico's insolence in hand, secured authorization from both houses of Congress for an armed intervention in Mexico. The total vote was 323 to 29. The US Navy attacked and occupied the port on April 22; in the process 126 Mexicans and 19 Americans were killed. US forces would remain until November 1914, a few months after Huerta's ouster.

Carranza immediately denounced the occupation on behalf of the Constitutionalists, while Villa publicly distanced himself from his chief and refused to criticize Wilson's action. It may have been that Villa had his sights on the presidency and guessed it would be hard to secure over US opposition. It may have also been a ploy to placate the gringos: why loudly provoke them as Carranza was doing? Better to ignore them and go about your business. No one knows for sure, but it was another example of Villa's very eclectic and changing political stances. He had a unique ability to pragmatically combine many positions, policies, and social forces in his camp, although it would ultimately be his undoing.

By spring 1914, cities and towns across the country were falling like dominoes to the Constitutionalists. Once again, the writing was on the wall. On July 15, 1914, Huerta resigned the presidency and fled Mexico. Carranza's forces entered the capital not long after, and the Constitutionalists were now officially masters of the country. The old Porfirian Federal Army had been decisively defeated; as an institution, it had been destroyed. A Venustiano Carranza presidency seemed to be close at hand, one charged with restoring the nation's constitutional order and ensuring a return to political stability.

But this was only in theory: the new masters were rife with internal divisions, as was Mexico as a whole. This soon led to a split in the Constitutionalist forces, and even further warfare. Why? In the next section we will take a closer look at the social and political composition of the Constitutionalists, why they broke apart, and why the forces of Villa and Zapata ultimately did not prevail.

3

1914–1920

General Victoriano Huerta had at last been driven from Mexican soil. It was 1914, and the motley rebel forces of the Constitutionalists and their allies were nominally in control of the country. Venustiano Carranza, their "First Chief," was planning to assume the presidency of Mexico. Indeed, this outcome had been explicitly written into the Constitutionalist program from the start.

Yet Carranza was a leader in name only. The opposition to Huerta was highly divided, beginning with Zapata's open mistrust of—if not hostility toward—the First Chief. These feelings, moreover, were clearly mutual. The divisions also extended to the rebel forces under Carranza's command, where Villa was increasingly asserting his independence from Carranza in military and political matters. In short, stability was not close at hand. The Constitutionalists would soon break apart, with several more years of civil war to come: Villa's and Zapata's forces would make up one camp, and Carranza and his supporters another.

Some historians attempt to explain these divisions as being simply about personal rivalries and an individual lust for power. From this perspective, Villa secretly coveted the presidential chair already reserved for Carranza, and Zapata and his forces for some (perhaps misguided) reason sided with Villa. The result was that their respective armies fought one another for several more years. Supporters of this view also note that the formal political programs of each faction came to converge to a large extent: Carranza, for example, eventually declared his support for land reform.

Yet this perspective misses form for substance. In particular, it overlooks the high level of political debate and contestation in the country, including within and between the revolutionary camps. From the start, as mentioned previously, Carranza had been challenged not only by the independent course of the Zapatistas but also by Villa, and by a radical wing within his own Constitutionalist forces. This wing was increasingly sympathetic to the Zapatistas' program of land redistribution, as well to carrying out other broad social reforms in Mexico, including expanding rights for the working class. Yet Carranza—given his landlord's outlook—was hostile to many of these proposals.

In late 1914, it seemed unlikely that Carranza's more conservative approach would prevail. Although he was still formally the leader of the Constitutionalists, in military and political terms he was the weaker party relative to Villa and Zapata. The person most associated with turning the conflict in Carranza's favor was one of his generals, the brilliant strategist Álvaro Obregón. He and many other young military officers, including a number of political radicals, ultimately chose to side with the First Chief despite his conservatism. They determined the strategy and rallied the forces that would bring victory to Carranza. These forces eventually included an important ally: the urban labor movement, particularly in Mexico City.

How did this come about? This question is the subject of the pages to follow. The ability of Carranza and his allies to prevail in the end was not simply a question of military strength, since at the start of the conflict Villa commanded the most feared and powerful army in Mexico. Rather, it depended in large part on the differences between Obregón's strategy and that pursued by Villa and Zapata. These in turn stemmed from differences in their respective political worldviews and goals.

In brief, many revolutionary military officers and their followers came to believe that Carranza's camp—or better put, Obregón's—was the one most capable of imposing a nationwide solution to the conflicts Mexico was facing. This meant defeating the Revolution's enemies across the country, and creating a strong central government once the dust settled. Moreover, they hoped to influence or even direct the course of that future government, so that it would carry out meaningful reforms nationally. Villa and Zapata did not seem up to these combined tasks.

In practice, Villa and Zapata were more focused on their own local and provincial affairs, rather than on a concrete plan for the nation as a whole. The Zapatistas' main interest was Morelos, more than the rest of Mexico. In Villa's case, his lack of concern with national political questions led to careless alliances, ones that weakened his camp and often strengthened the hand of his enemies. In all, this made it difficult for both leaders to carry out their aims on a broader scale. In contrast, Obregón thought about the broader national dimension from the very start.

Yet on whatever scale, for Villa's and Zapata's supporters the key question remained whether the social changes to come would happen under the watchful eye of armed campesinos. They did not trust Carranza or anyone who would follow him. Without their forces calling the shots, agrarian radicals like Zapata believed that Carranza would not press for land reform and would attempt to undermine any gains already made. They ended up being right.

The Roots of the Great Revolutionary Split

As Huerta's regime tottered, Carranza found himself caught between two poles. While he clearly wanted to topple the dictatorship, and push out the old Porfirian political elite, he did not want to give in to armed campesinos' demands for land. These demands, however, showed no sign of abating. It was abundantly clear that campesino initiatives were not being restrained by the relatively limited program—the Plan de Guadalupe—that had been officially issued by the Constitutionalists. The key point of contention, as it had been with Madero, continued to be land reform. This was something Carranza steadfastly opposed, yet he encountered strong dissent across the country on this issue, including within his own Constitutionalist ranks.

One early case, during the war against Huerta, made this tension clear. Lucio Blanco, one of Carranza's young officers, had distributed lands from a confiscated hacienda in the northern state of Tamaulipas, accompanied by a great deal of speechmaking about the importance of agrarian reform. In response, Carranza publicly censured Blanco soon after, and transferred him from his post. According to the First Chief, there would be no taking away of the landlords' "legally sanctioned rights" in order to hand over their property to those "who do not have the right."[1]

Yet Lucio Blanco was not an isolated case of internal dissent from Carranza's program. Shortly after Huerta's defeat, Carranza ordered another of his Constitutionalist officers to return a confiscated hacienda in San Luis Potosí to its owners. The officer's response to the First Chief is instructive:

> The Espinosa y Parra [family] are part of a group of hacendados from San Luis Potosí whose fortunes cannot be considered legitimately acquired capital, . . . it cannot be considered capital resulting from legitimate profit which the hacendados acquired after having paid their workers just salaries, but on the contrary the fortune of these individuals as that of the majority of hacendados . . . is in my humble opinion nothing but the salary that these hacendados should have paid their workers. It is these workers who produced the merchandise which has made the hacendados rich and which has allowed them to have palaces . . . while the humble workers on their haciendas . . . don't even have pants to cover their nakedness nor do they have shoes to wear and they are the main producers of national wealth.[2]

For Carranza, however, Zapatismo represented something even more dangerous than the agrarian radicalism infecting many of his subordinates. They were operating completely independently of his authority, attacking haciendas, and carrying out land reform on the spot, without delay. Given the First Chief's views, it's not surprising that he regarded the distribution of land to campesinos under Zapata as simply an illegal act, one to be stopped, if not punished. Indeed, while the war against Huerta was in progress, a Zapatista delegation to Carranza—with the radical agrarian Plan de Ayala in hand—was pointedly rebuffed. The First Chief reportedly informed Zapata's emissaries that "this land-redistribution business is absurd. Tell me which haciendas you own and are able to redistribute, so that each of you can redistribute what belongs to you, rather than what belongs to someone else."[3] Historian Adolfo Gilly describes the significance of this exchange for both parties: "Genovevo de la O [Zapata's emissary] had risen in armed revolt with twenty-five men and a single rifle: he was a campesino then, and would still be a campesino when he died in the 1950s. The man who had the perfidy and insolence to ask which haciendas he had to redistribute was himself a big Coahuila landowner."[4]

Soon after, Carranza's internal communiqués began to refer to Zapata's forces as simply "the enemy."[5] Zapata undoubtedly viewed the First Chief in the same light. For those committed to land reform, it was more and more evident that a closed, centralized regime composed of Carranza and his most conservative allies would not bode well for Mexico's campesinos. Moreover, this was not merely a question of land reform in the future: there was also the question of the land seizures and land distribution that had already taken place, and were currently taking place, in Morelos. As with Madero, not only would Carranza refuse to carry out land reform; he would also order campesinos to give back land they had already taken, tilled, and planted.

This was a question that extended far beyond Morelos, since campesinos were in revolt in various other parts of Mexico as well. In San Luis Potosí, for example, the famed Cedillo brothers had rebelled on behalf of agrarian reform since the days of Madero's presidency. Their family had long been considered an advocate for the poor in the region, and the uprising began when sixty share-croppers from the surrounding haciendas arrived at their home and demanded that the Cedillos lead them into battle. They rose up against the Maderista state government, capturing several towns and reading the Plan de Ayala aloud to the assembled townsfolk. By the fall of Huerta it was estimated that more than five thousand rebels had taken up arms across San Luis Potosí, the bulk of them under the Cedillos, although there were some thirty-four different bands in all.[6]

In the state of Durango, the agrarian radical Calixto Contreras also had a strong following, leading four to five thousand troops who fought with Villa against the Huerta regime. Under Madero—despite having fought for the young president—Contreras had been labeled a "danger to the state of Durango" and thrown in jail in Mexico City, escaping just before the Huerta coup. By the time of Huerta's fall he was the main power in his home state and in the rebellious Laguna region. For Zapata, Contreras was "a son of the humble people and a fighter for the land" as well as "the revolutionary from the north that inspires the most confidence." In Contreras's domains the haciendas had nearly all been sacked, and grassroots agrarian distribution was under way.[7]

Elsewhere, in Tamaulipas, agrarian rebels battled Carranza's newly appointed governor, a wealthy hacendado uninterested in land reform. They were led by Alberto Carrera Torres, a rural schoolteacher, and his brother Francisco; their forces also worked closely with the Cedillos in neighboring San Luis Potosí. The two camps issued a joint twenty-point manifesto calling for agrarian reform in the region. Another hotbed of campesino activity was found in the adjoining states of Tlaxcala and Puebla, where Domingo Arenas and his brothers had joined forces with Zapata. They put the Plan de Ayala into practice in their area of operations, distributing lands as hacendados fled their estates in terror. In the state of Guerrero the dominant rebel leader was Jesús Salgado, who had also recently signed on to the Plan de Ayala. This was un-known to Carranza, however, and he appointed Salgado to be gov-ernor of the state after Huerta's fall. Immediately following his appointment Salgado publicly declared his allegiance to Zapata, undoubtedly flustering and frustrating the First Chief.[8]

Militarily speaking, however, it was Pancho Villa who repre-sented the most immediate potential threat to Carranza. Villa was an immensely popular figure and led the most powerful single armed force in Mexico, the fearsome Northern Division. In Chi-huahua, as with Morelos, a key question was what do with the land not only in the future but in the present. That is, what was to be done with the property that had *already* been confiscated, mainly from landlords who had supported Huerta and the Federal Army? The fate of this land was a major issue for Villa and his supporters. Carranza had tolerated these land seizures, but only if they were carried out against political enemies and used to fund the rebellion. What Carranza would not accept was the eventual redistribution of this same land to Villa's rank-and-file soldiers. His plan was to return it to its original owners once the conflict was over, or per-haps sell it to new investors. The presence of campesinos squatting on this land and tilling it—likely with arms in hand—would make this goal near-impossible. Moreover, it would only raise the expec-tations of campesinos elsewhere.

Villa, as noted earlier, was never strongly ideological. But as

a popular caudillo, he firmly believed in taking care of "his people."
Carranza's consolidating his power, and the way he would use that
power, would be an obstacle to Villa's playing this role. Put differently, Villa wanted the power to decide matters in his own
backyard; as president, Carranza would be an obstacle to this, and
to carrying out social change more generally. At minimum, Villa
envisioned distributing land to his men, or their widows, when
the fighting was over. Indeed, it would be almost inconceivable
for Villa to betray his soldiers—to disgrace himself, in effect—by
voluntarily conceding on this point. But Carranza's own views
were increasingly clear: the First Chief had already appointed a
governor in Chihuahua who was unfriendly to Villa, and he demanded that Villa begin to return expropriated property. Again,

Pancho Villa (center) reviewing his troops

this was a near-impossibility: handing back the land seized from the hated magnate Luis Terrazas, for example, was simply not an option for Villa.

On the eve of Huerta's defeat, Villa and Carranza's disagreements had finally come to a boil, with Carranza blocking deliveries of coal and ammunition to Villa's troops. The two men tried to make peace with the so-called Torreón Pact, negotiated by way of emissaries. The pact reaffirmed that Villa and the Northern Division were subordinate to Carranza's command. However, in a concession to Villa, the accord also stipulated that "the present struggle pits the powerless against the powerful," and that the goals of its signatories included "the economic emancipation of the proletariat through an equitable distribution of land, and by securing the welfare of the industrial workers." Yet neither Villa nor Carranza liked the pact. Villa didn't trust Carranza, and didn't want to remain under his authority. Carranza, meanwhile, had no intention of honoring the pact's more radical provisions. Ultimately neither party adhered to it.

The conflicts between Villa and Carranza, and the dissent among many of Carranza's officers, did not escape Zapata's notice. In 1913, he sent an emissary to meet with Villa and became convinced of the latter's commitment to agrarian reform. Although Villa did not make any formal proclamations on the subject, his attacks on the property of landlords and the rich in Chihuahua had made his sympathies clear, as far as Zapata was concerned. Moreover, Villa's opposition to Carranza's bid for power, and his criticisms of Carranza's positions on land reform, brought their alliance closer together, even if from afar. The stage had been set for a fight.

Obregón and the Revolutionary "Jacobins"

Following the defeat of Huerta, the Constitutionalists were hardly unaware of their differences: they organized a "revolutionary Convention" to hopefully resolve them. It was called to order in October 1914 in the center-north city of Aguascalientes, three months after the dictator Huerta's ouster. Carranza had in fact been forced to agree to the gathering: his preferred scenario was that he assume the presidency directly, with no debate or dissent among his forces. But this scenario was clearly no longer possible.

The overwhelming majority of delegates to the Convention were military officers from the various revolutionary armies. They constituted an important and relatively independent camp, even if technically speaking their loyalty lay with Carranza, their First Chief. Their most notable representative was Álvaro Obregón, the Constitutionalists' most successful and popular general after Villa. Although at this stage Obregón was outshined by more prominent figures like Villa and Zapata, he would come to play a crucial role in the later years of the Revolution. He would also emerge as the last man standing in the end, and would assume the presidency of Mexico in 1920. But this was still several years and many battles away.

The Convention was not expected to be a celebratory event. By the time it began, the Torreón Pact between Villa and Carranza had already collapsed; according to Villa, this was due to Carranza's treachery and his refusal to adhere to the pact's terms. Villa had thus repudiated the First Chief's command, and the Northern Division was now an authority unto itself under Villa's leadership. As a condition for his participation in the Convention, Villa demanded that land reform be placed explicitly on the agenda. This was agreed to. Meanwhile, Carranza's other opponents also arrived: the Zapatistas, who had remained initially aloof, eventually sent representatives. Their delegation was received with great fanfare, much to Carranza's dismay. Their principal spokesmen in this period were two young anarchist-influenced intellectuals who had committed themselves to the Zapatista cause: Manuel Palafox and Antonio Díaz Soto y Gama.

In the end, Carranza would emerge the loser at the Convention. The body adopted left-wing positions on a range of issues, under the influence of the radicals in its midst. The Convention pledged to address the country's "deep social needs," rather than limit itself to the narrow set of changes Carranza sought. Zapata's representatives won over a majority of the body to agrarian reform, and it voted to support the Plan de Ayala. At minimum this meant a commitment to the restitution of village lands, and the destruction of large landholdings. The setbacks to Carranza would not end there: the Convention soon declared itself a sovereign body and announced its intention to form a government, thus nullifying the First Chief's presidential aspirations. Carranza—not surprisingly—continued to challenge the Convention's authority, and was finally declared to be in revolt.

And so the next phase of the armed conflict had begun: the question was which side people would choose. The delegates—the rebel military officers—faced a decision following the Convention: Carranza was a landlord, personally hungry for power and clearly committed to limiting change in Mexico. Villa and Zapata were the representatives of the dispossessed campesino and plebeian forces in the Revolution, and were pressing change forward. At first blush, the choice would seem obvious—and many agrarian leaders and radical reformers in fact went with Villa and Zapata. Lucio Blanco, the aforementioned military officer who attempted land reform against Carranza's wishes, was one of these.

Yet interestingly, many delegates at the Convention ended up siding with Carranza rather than Zapata and Villa in the end. This took place in spite of the latters' popularity and the Convention's support for their positions. Why? Understanding this requires returning to the various motivations for taking part in the Revolution discussed earlier in this book and how they influenced the participants at this crucial point.

First, it is important to realize that many of the revolutionary military officers present at the Convention were not veterans of agrarian reform movements, nor did they necessarily come from poor campesino villages. We should remember that (along with agrarian conflict) a key motive force in the Revolution was the way the previous regime has severely restricted the prospects of Mexico's middle classes for political and economic advancement. Those who identified with this perspective were also represented at the Convention. They did not share the visceral land hunger that characterized Zapata's movement, nor its egalitarian philosophy.[9]

Nonetheless, many among the Constitutionalist officers had also been radicalized by the tragic fate of President Madero, and the recent experience of several years of agrarian revolt. They were moving beyond the long-standing ideal of Liberal government reform that had been championed by the murdered president. They had become sympathetic to proposals for more profound change, including land redistribution and expanding labor rights. In addition, it was becoming increasingly clear to them that for Mexico to progress and carry out these important reforms, the entrenched privileges of the past had to be broken, and especially those of the landlord class. General Álvaro Obregón could be said to fit this profile, along with a number of other revolutionary officers.

What kind of radicals were they? They were not necessarily opposed to capitalism, but were certainly disgusted with the privileged Porfirian capitalists that Mexico had endured for decades. They did not believe that either campesinos or workers should govern the country—such a role was reserved for people like themselves—but they did believe that campesinos and workers should be granted significant reforms. Contemporaries called these radical reformers "Jacobins," a reference to the radical middle-class camp in the French Revolution.

Their support for the campesinos would have its limits, however. The Mexican Jacobins' middle-class vision of change still called for it to be carried out from the top down, by the enlightened few, via legalistic, administrative means. They were never very keen on the campesinos' unruly and unrestrained approach to reform. Showing up at the hacienda, shooting the administrator, and freely distributing the land—this was out of line. The appropriate decrees had to be issued, documents signed, agricultural engineers consulted. Villa and Zapata's provincial campesino and plebeian forces were not the vehicle that could create a nationwide apparatus to carry out orderly, systematic change directed from above. Moreover, when Carranza radicalized his own program soon after the Convention—declaring his support for land distribution and labor rights—the middle-class "instincts" of the Jacobins pulled them closer to the elite Carranza and away from the coarse and undisciplined armed campesinos.

It would be more accurate to say, in fact, that they were drawn to Carranza's general, Álvaro Obregón. It was he who impelled Carranza to significantly change his program, against the narrow-minded hacendado's own wishes. As historian Adolfo Gilly has noted, the success of Obregón's approach "depended on the partial incorporation of its enemy's [Villa's and Zapata's] program."[10] The point, however, was not only to defeat Villa and Zapata. Presidents Díaz, Madero, and Huerta had tried this—basing themselves on a program of status quo for the wealthy elite—and failed. For Obregón the goal was also to break the other enemy: the old Porfirian landlords and their allies.

To do this required mobilizing the support of workers and campesinos by granting them significant concessions. Obregón

Álvaro Obregón, the Constitutionalist general

sought to build a strong, centralized national regime that could bring an end to the revolutionary upheaval, grant social reforms to the masses across the country (to not do so, as Carranza wished, would be political suicide), and reestablish a Mexican capitalist economy on a sounder basis. All this also meant crushing the resistance of the remaining reactionary elements of Porfirian society, who had continued to exert their influence under both Madero and Huerta. For Obregón and his radical Jacobin allies, the forces of Villa and Zapata would not be able to accomplish these ambitious goals.

Moreover, Zapatismo posed a political threat to the Jacobins' program. The Morelos campesinos had their own independent revolutionary agenda for the land, and were carrying out change from below, on their own initiative, not under the direction and control of any outside authority. Zapata also had a powerful military ally in Villa. Ultimately, despite their differences with Carranza, Obregón, and

Álvaro Obregón, the politician

many other radicals made their choice following the Convention: while significant social reform was needed in Mexico, it could only happen from the top down, by means of a strong national government. Only this could guarantee a return to social stability.

So who was the savvy and influential Obregón? He was already thirty-three years old when he joined the fight against Huerta, with a background as a small-scale commercial farmer and entrepreneur. Obregón was from Sonora, a booming northern state that had developed—likely more than any other region in Mexico—that mobile, entrepreneurial, ambitious (and angry) middle class that characterizes many expanding capitalist economies. But his relatively humble origins and work experience meant that he, unlike the aristocratic Carranza, was not that far removed from the country people he led. He spoke a bit of Yaqui and Mayo, the languages of the indigenous people in Sonora, and recruited their bowmen and scouts into his forces, while others scoffed. Obregón had also had military successes fighting against Huerta, mainly in the northwest, but he was far more cautious and deliberate than the more audacious Villa. Indeed, unlike Villa, whose approach to combat was often improvised, Obregón became an avid student of military strategy and tactics. And while Villa had the grassroots appeal of the tough plebeian bandit, Obregón was the populist self-made man who could also rally his troops and command their respect.

While somewhat cautious in terms of military strategy, Obregón often displayed considerable audacity in the area of political maneuvering. Prior to the Convention, for example, Obregón went directly to Villa's headquarters in Chihuahua City—with an escort of only twenty men—to try to resolve the conflict with Carranza. It was a risky move: Villa not only was angry with Carranza (and anyone associated with him) but was also a highly unpredictable character. And in fact, Obregón almost lost his life in this effort, not once but twice.

Obregón was welcomed at first, and saluted by an honor guard at Villa's headquarters. Together he and Villa drafted a proposal to Carranza calling for agrarian reform and insisting that Carranza occupy the presidency only on a temporary basis, in the interest of peace. By removing Carranza from the picture, Obregón was likely trying to open the door to his own future ambitions as well. Obregón left Villa's headquarters with their joint proposal in hand, but it went nowhere—Carranza rejected it outright. In response, Obregón decided to make another risky trip to negotiate with Villa. In part, he also wished to assess the loyalty of Villa's generals and civilian supporters. At this point Villa suspected treachery by Obregón, and shortly after his arrival Villa confronted him and ordered him shot. While Obregón awaited his fate, Villa changed his mind, under pressure from some of his own generals. Obregón was invited to a dance, and the following day the two men hammered out another proposal to Carranza, similar to the first. Carranza rejected this one as well, and ordered that the rail lines between Chihuahua City and his own headquarters be cut. Furious, Villa once again ordered that Obregón, as Carranza's messenger, be shot. This time, however, the wily general was able to escape, in part with help from some of Villa's officers. Meanwhile, he had kept his cool throughout and had used the whole affair to assess the state of Villa's forces, determine the political inclinations of his officer corps, and weaken the loyalty of some of them for the tempestuous Villa.

Villa and Obregón had thus come to know each other well, and would eventually face one another on the battlefield in a series of clashes that were crucial to the outcome of the Revolution. This direct confrontation would come later, however: following the Convention, Zapata and Villa were the clear victors. Carranza, Obregón, and their troops—now officially in revolt—retreated from the capital toward the coastal city of Veracruz. The city was eventually handed to them by the departing US occupation forces. It was another step in a clumsy US policy: although Washington did not want Carranza as president due to his nationalist inclinations, it also wanted a counterweight to a potential future President Villa. In the end almost nothing the US government did turned out as it expected or wished.

With their rivals in retreat, Villa and Zapata met for the first time, in the town of Xochimilco, just south of Mexico City. Their combined forces then entered the nation's capital, under the banner of the Convention. It was surely the high point of the campesino struggle during the Revolution. But Carranza and Obregón's forces were far from defeated, even as they fled to the coast. They had maintained the support of a portion of the Constitutionalist camp, and over time they would win over more. A key remaining potential ally was urban labor, and particularly the increasingly organized working class in Mexico City. Crucially, Obregón saw this clearly, whereas Villa and Zapata did not. The former was able to secure urban workers' allegiance to his banner, whereas the campesino wing of the Revolution failed to. This political development helped tip the overall balance of the conflict in Mexico.

Nationalism and Provincialism in the Revolutionary Camps

Over the course of 1915, Mexico City would change hands various times as both factions jockeyed for position and territory. One such occasion was especially significant. In February 1915, before he was engaged in direct action against Villa, Obregón briefly retook Mexico City from Villa and Zapata's Convention government. During this period he obtained the political and military support of the main trade union federation in the capital, along with that of other labor organizations. That is, he quickly accomplished something that Villa and Zapata could not do—or would not do—in the time they had held the capital. Moreover, these organized trade union workers marched with Obregón by the thousands to fight Villa on the battlefield.

How did this happen? Obregón was certainly politically astute, but it was hardly due to this fact alone. Ultimately, the strategy taken by either side reflected the overall political outlook that characterized them and their leaders. The key was that one camp—the forces of Villa and Zapata—held to a parochial or provincial perspective, one focused on local or regional affairs over national ones. What occurred beyond their respective provincial confines was not as politically significant to them. The other camp—Obregón's and Carranza's—had a national perspective, focused on carrying out their program throughout the whole country and constructing a political means to this end.

Villa and Zapata had a track record of opposition to the landlords, broader grassroots support, and—by extension—more men under arms. But their parochial outlook made it very difficult for them, in various ways, to carry out their agenda on a wider scale. In contrast, the rump Constitutionalist camp was able to translate its national perspective into a more effective political and military force. Put simply, Obregón could tell potential allies—including the labor movement—something along these lines: "We will promise specific reforms to you; we will implement them where we have power; we will make these changes happen nationwide; and we will ultimately back them up with legal, governmental authority." The zeal and effectiveness of the radical Jacobin officers around Obregón made these promises seem like more than just words. Villa and Zapata might have had the means to pursue this more ambitious road, but they did not have the political inclination. In what follows we consider why.

The first question to address is where this political provincialism came from. On the one hand, it reflected one of the key motive forces of the Revolution already discussed: a desire for local control, regional autonomy, and an end to central government interference. This was, in short, the politics of "leave us alone"—and it meant a lack of concern with national political questions and government. Ambitious national programs of reform, of whatever stripe, carried with them the likelihood of increased meddling by the national state. Many rural people, accustomed to the decades of how this operated under the Porfirian dictatorship, wanted none of it. And they were well represented in Villa's camp. For them, it was better to fight for the right to manage one's own affairs within the *patria chica*, the small homeland.

Political parochialism also reflected the nature of rural campesino life of the era. The day-to-day focus was very often on the land, soil, rainfall, planting, and harvest. When this life was under threat, campesinos in Mexico had shown they were capable of tremendous political radicalism, best represented by Zapatista Morelos. But leaders of volunteer campesino armies— like the Zapatistas—also had to recognize that major offensives could not happen at planting and harvest times. The campesinos' way of life consistently pulled them back to the patria chica. For them what happened in Mexico City should, in the best of circumstances, be of little or no concern.

Even Zapata himself—by now a nationally recognized figure—had little interest in political affairs in Mexico City. He remained in the capital only briefly, staying at a modest hotel near the train station, and declined to address the crowds gathered to hear speeches at the National Palace. In short, city politics and urban society were a largely foreign place for the Morelos campesinos, Zapata included. In one noted incident, Zapatista soldiers, approached by a fire engine in the capital, attacked it—they mistook the giant red truck, its bells ringing, for a machine of war.[11]

In strategic terms, for the Zapatista forces the occupation of the capital after the Convention was not a first step toward creating and administering a national regime. Taking Mexico City was merely a step to beat back the forces that would not let them carry out land reform as they wished in Morelos. The campesino troops, whose struggle focused on their local villages, did not want to fight—or legislate—far from them. The historian Friedrich Katz has described Zapatismo as "well-nigh invincible at its center, but virtually ineffectual beyond its confines."[12] Put differently, the Zapatistas were like the sports team that performs exceedingly well at home but poorly on the road. This was true of other agrarian movements as well.

Obregón's agenda differed in this respect: it was all about winning on the road. This meant not focusing on one "home" region but aggressively exporting the Constitutionalist agenda to various parts of the republic. According to historian Alan Knight, for the Zapatistas the occupation of Mexico City was "a painful necessity, dictated by the strategic needs of Morelos."[13] For Obregón's camp, the eventual taking of Morelos by force was also a painful necessity, dictated by the strategic needs of national power.

In the case of Pancho Villa, he probably wanted more than anything to simply return home: to live as a popular caudillo, a benevolent patron for the people of Chihuahua. He fought against the obstacles to this goal, not for national power. With his hopes for "his people" satisfied, Villa would gladly have left government to the men in starched collars. Then he could settle into a nice ranch, devoting himself to raising horses and trading war stories—which for a time, toward the end of his life, he did.

But to do this Villa had to defeat his enemies. His approach was a very pragmatic one: assemble the largest army possible. In confronting Carranza, Villa gathered whatever forces of various political stripes would ally themselves to him; he didn't seem to mind who jumped on board. He wouldn't require them to personally support the kinds of radical changes he had made in Chihuahua. Villa believed he could command them all via his successful military leadership and personal charisma, rather than by means of any particular ideology or political program.

Yet this lack of a consistent worldview was increasingly a weakness. It meant that Villa's movement would eventually become a grab-bag of contradictory elements, united only by their opposition to Carranza and Obregón. The alliance even came to include a number of firm opponents of social reform, including northern landlords who were political rivals of Carranza, representatives of the Church who feared the anticlerical bent of Obregón and his followers, and even former Federal Army officers. Indeed, though they had been given no quarter by Villa during the fight against Huerta, former Porfirian officers were now welcomed into his camp. A former Federal, Felipe Ángeles, soon became Villa's most prominent military adviser. While Ángeles was a clearly a brilliant officer and artilleryman, for much of his life he had been no friend of land reform and social radicalism. Ultimately, these more conservative elements hoped to ride the Villista horse to political influence once the dust settled. Meanwhile, Carranza and Obregón were able to paint Villa as a "reactionary" among potential allies—such as the urban working class—mainly for having allowed so many dubious figures into his ranks.

Villa also had the support of a number of agrarian radicals, from early on. But despite Villa's sympathies for the less fortunate, he did not base his movement on a clear commitment to agrarian reform, nor any sort of egalitarian worldview, like that provided by the Zapatistas' Plan de Ayala. Some of his officers and generals were headed in the other direction, in fact: they began personally enriching themselves through the control of expropriated properties in Chihuahua and beyond. While some of the money generated from these properties went to the Northern Division, some of it also went into the generals' own pockets. Although they were hostile to the old Porfirian landlords—given that they were now sitting on their land—such figures would not be among those pressing for agrarian reform. Ultimately, these ambitious Villista generals had aspirations to become successful ranchers, if not large landowners in their own right, when the conflict was over.

There was yet another limitation to Villa's carrying out aggressive land reform. Unlike Zapata's forces, who stayed close to their home region—usually close enough to return home for the harvest—Villa's soldiers were part of a highly mobile army. Villa was unwilling to carry out land reform on behalf of those who had stayed behind and not joined the fight with him. He wanted the reform to benefit his soldiers, as well as their widows and orphans—that is, his people. All this had to wait until the war with Carranza was over.

Villa's troops, moreover, did not have the close ties to local village communities, hungry for land, that were the foundation of Zapata's movement. Among Villa's soldiers were former ranch hands, muleteers, unemployed miners, cowboys, street peddlers, and the urban poor—that is, people who had never held a piece of land of their own.[14] Land was not, and had not been, the basis of their immediate survival or that of their families. Friedrich Katz has noted on the question of land reform, "Where there was consistency in the [Zapatista] South, there was ambivalence in the [Villista] North."[15] What was a question of immediate urgency for Zapata's troops was not for Villa's.

In the end, there was a growing lack of a clear shared purpose among the motley components of Villa's movement. It meant that the principal thing uniting them was Villa himself, and what he could provide them. Villa was undoubtedly aware of this, and it did not seem to faze him. But this "broad church" approach would eventually come to undermine his camp. Its extremely mixed political makeup meant that it could not agree on many things, aside from defeating Carranza and Obregón. Eventually it could not develop or carry out any kind of unified policy beyond a military one. The movement's internal divisions would also come to paralyze the new Convention government.

The inconsistent and unstable politics of Villismo were at a further disadvantage when it came to the battle for hearts and minds against Obregón's forces. The latter were increasingly focused on carrying out a concrete set of social reforms across the country. Thus while Villa continued to haphazardly broaden his camp, Obregón focused his program and honed its effectiveness. Obregón's first concern wasn't the size of his coalition or his army. It was its adherence to a consistent political agenda. He wanted a force that could carry out certain political objectives nationwide and ultimately take and hold national power.

Thus despite the setback at the Convention, Obregón soon took the military and political initiative. Case in point: in early 1915, the Constitutionalists assembled armies and dispatched them to some of the more remote southern states of the republic—Tabasco, Yucatán, and Chiapas. The forces were led by some of their most radical Jacobin officers: Francisco Múgica, Salvador Alvarado, and Jesús Agustín Castro. The far south of the country had seen little revolutionary upheaval; in certain regions, campesinos labored on haciendas under semi-slave conditions of debt bondage. Here, rather than make deals with local elite interests and power brokers, the Constitutionalists attempted to break them, and gain support among the rural and urban poor. In regions they conquered, the Jacobins abolished debt bondage, minimum wages were set, forced loans were levied on the rich, public works and education projects were established, old *caciques* (political bosses) were jailed, land distribution programs were initiated, and trade unions and peasant associations were set up and supported—as long as they remained loyal to the new regime. As Alvarado famously declared regarding the Yucatán campesinos, "Give them lands, and we bind them to Mexico." He would later argue that the only way to build a strong national state was to "organize these Indians, creating real interests for them which they owe to the Revolution."[16]

The taking of the Yucatán, meanwhile, guaranteed a steady stream of cash for the Constitutionalist coffers, due to the region's high export revenues. The same was true when the Constitutionalists took the gulf port of Tampico, a major center of oil production. Following the above pattern, Tampico was successfully held not by gaining the support of the oil and shipping companies, but by granting major concessions to the city's oil and dockworkers unions. Taxes on oil exports were increased, rising from less than half a million pesos annually to more than twelve million, further filling the Consitutionalist war chest.

A key next step would be to take this approach to Mexico City. However, the first ones to occupy the capital were Villa and Zapata, under the banner of the Convention, fresh from having ousted Carranza and his allies. At this stage the differences in outlook and strategy between the two rival camps would start to become more clear.

Hearts and Minds in Mexico City: Villa and Zapata

Zapata and Villa's forces triumphantly entered Mexico City in December 1914, and the victorious Convention quickly established a new government. Soon the Convention would be put to the test of building wider alliances, carrying out reforms, and helping a population desperately seeking to meet its basic needs. Yet this new government—despite the many radical proclamations at Aguascalientes—frequently stumbled in carrying out these tasks. Why? Here we need to look at the approach of the Villa and Zapata camps, which taken together constituted the military and political backbone of the Convention.

Almost immediately, the new Convention government faced the problem that it was internally fractured. When it came time to put forward and implement concrete reforms, including around land distribution, the more conservative wing of Villa's extremely broad movement was a continuous obstacle. The Zapatista left wing maneuvered, argued, and wrangled with its opponents within the Convention. But the concrete result was that there was no unified political direction coming from the new government. It was, in effect, a debating society set up in the midst of a civil war, and it quickly fell into disarray and ineffectiveness. Surprisingly—if not shockingly—it took the Convention more than a year to promulgate a nationwide land reform law, by which time its armies had already been put to rout. It would disband shortly thereafter. Obregón was able to secure such a decree within his camp within a few weeks.

Moreover, when the Convention did issue laws and decrees, it couldn't really enforce them. The Convention was unable to develop effective political, administrative, or military resources of its own. The bulk of the Convention's military forces—under Villa and Zapata—soon returned to Morelos and Chihuahua. Rather than carrying out reforms in Mexico City or furthering a national political agenda, they focused on reinforcing their home bases. Indeed, Zapata and Villa were so uninterested in questions of urban politics that they simply handed over various duties in the capital to past Porfirian officials and bureaucrats, including the former chief of police. In one case, when a demonstration of working-class women came to the Convention government demanding relief and bread, all the delegates were able to do was to take up a personal collection among themselves. For the insecure laborers and hungry poor of the capital, a government whose officials had to fish around in their pockets to help them was simply not an effective government.

Another factor limiting working-class support for the Convention was the chaotic nature of Villista authority in the capital. This was connected, in part, to the lack of adherence to a clear ideal or worldview in Villa's camp. A layer of Villa's troops and officers had become increasingly professionalized, even mercenary. They obeyed Villa's command, but fought for a meal, salary, and the occasional booty, not any higher purpose, other than their personal advantage. This led to a form of arbitrary, lawless rule when Villa's troops were billeted in Mexico City. Villa's "rowdies" went on repeated rampages in the capital, principally directed against the rich. Homes were ransacked and looted, wine cellars emptied, hotels and restaurants trashed, cars seized and taken on joyrides— all accompanied by a great deal of shooting and revelry. Wealthy residents were kidnapped and extorted for ransom, and a significant number of summary executions took place. Even Villa himself got in on the act, at one point jailing the French owner of a prominent hotel—and causing a minor diplomatic crisis in the process— for sheltering an attractive cashier Villa wished to seduce.

In short, while Villa and his officers were clearly hostile to the old Porfirian upper crust, they were not especially concerned, politically speaking, with support from Mexico City workers or the poor. They were antigovernment rebels, but as mentioned, they were not consistently animated by an egalitarian outlook. Moreover, although Villa himself maintained a materially austere lifestyle, a good number of his officers were highly acquisitive and self-seeking. In a sense, they held on to a significant aspect of the contemporary middle-class worldview: the powerful ambition for individual self-advancement, unrestrained by others. Thus while some of the lawless Villista behavior could be characterized as the lower classes seeking to settle scores with the Porfirian rich, a large part of it was a product of mere covetousness and greed.

None of this helped the Villistas win many supporters among the urban working class and the poor. It was not that the latter had much sympathy for the old elite. But in a city increasingly beset by hunger, lack of fuel, and overall insecurity, the lawlessness of Villa's officers stoked fears among many beyond just the well-off. Most importantly, kidnapping or shooting a few wealthy people for their money was not part of a clearly articulated policy that could actually help the poor and the working class—and they likely recognized this. Obregón, in contrast, would take a very different approach when he was in charge in the capital.

Concern with the ineffectiveness and disorganization of the Convention, and Villa's relatively chaotic authority, grew among some of its own officials as well. A number of them—including prominent military officers and intellectuals—finally defected to Obregón, drawn to his seemingly more systematic and effective strategy for reform. In other cases, they merely feared the rough frontier justice meted out by Villa's forces. One example, that of José Vasconcelos, an attorney and intellectual drawn to Villismo, is somewhat illustrative. Vasconcelos would go on to become one of Mexico's most prominent twentieth-century men of letters, but during the Revolution he was just another literate man who lent his services to Villa's movement. He was appointed minister of education once the Convention was established in Mexico City, but he soon faced a serious dilemma. One of Villa's generals held a powerful grudge against him. Vasconcelos had allegedly taken extensive legal fees from the general back when he was a simple campesino facing trial, and had then left the man to rot in jail. The general's solution was simple: Vasconcelos had to be given a good thrashing, if not shot. Villa apparently agreed. Vasconcelos finally fled and joined Obregón, rather than face a possible summary execution.

The Zapatistas played a somewhat different role in the capital. As mentioned, the Morelos campesinos were out of their element in Mexico City and not especially concerned with its affairs. Nonetheless, they were reported to be both humble and respectful of its residents. This was in large part because their worldview took them in a different direction from that of Villa's more self-serving followers. The Zapatistas' struggle was closely connected with the fate of their villages: their goal was defending and preserving each village as an organized community, in possession of land. Thus the well-being of any one campesino was seen as integrally tied to that of others in the village and the broader movement. This accounted for the Zapatistas' determined sense of common purpose and collective solidarity.[17] But this solidarity did not easily extend to other social groups, and they retreated from questions of urban or national politics at the first opportunity.

Mexico City's urban working class was thus apparently left without a consistent ally among the revolutionary camps. At least that seemed to be the case until Obregón returned to the nation's capital and sought to make himself their champion.

Hearts and Minds in Mexico City: Obregón

Where Villa and Zapata were often politically uninterested in the labor movement and the poor of Mexico City, Obregón consciously wooed them. He appeared to be far more attuned to day-to-day working-class concerns in the city. Upon retaking the capital in February 1915, he quickly set up a Revolutionary Junta for Aid to the Public, to distribute food and cash relief. To fund the effort, half a million pesos was immediately demanded from the Catholic Church and a similarly large sum from the wealthy businessmen of the capital. When both groups balked, their representatives were summoned to a meeting at the National Palace and immediately placed under arrest. The Church, Obregón told the capital's residents, "which gave forty million to the execrable assassin Victoriano Huerta, . . . today has not even half a million for our needy classes."[18] Food speculators and price gougers were also arrested, and made to sweep the city's streets. This approach was a step ahead of Villista "rowdyism"—Obregón was using his military strength to institutionalize popular, immediate political changes at gunpoint. Meanwhile, the Zapatistas and the Convention leadership responded to Obregón's retaking of Mexico City by attacking and cutting off the capital's water supplies—a potential disaster for the urban poor in terms of thirst and disease.[19] Such a step would not increase the popular support for their camp.

Obregón's greatest coup, however, was with the Mexico City labor unions. The most significant alliance he forged during his brief stay in the capital was with its main labor federation, the Casa del Obrero Mundial (House of the Global Worker).* The Casa is

---

* This name is also frequently translated as "House of the World Worker."

often described as an anarcho-syndicalist organization: this is over-stated, but its publications and a number of its early leaders were influenced by contemporary anarchist doctrine. It was founded in 1912 as an organization largely composed of skilled workers and artisans, and intended as a "Center for the Doctrinaire Dissemination of Advanced Ideas." The Casa had an initial focus on education and cultural improvement, something that characterized many organizations among skilled laborers at this time. Working-class attendees at its early events often wore formal attire. Notably, the Casa was also a strong advocate of gender equality. Although few women became part of its leadership, women were freely admitted into its courses and were not limited to studying variants of home economics. Women also served as instructors, where they promoted a "scientific and rational" outlook concerning the equality of men and women. Along with education, the Casa soon began advocating "direct action" by workers and a rejection of any involvement in political activity, as befitted the anarchist influence within it. That said, as a movement it still had little experience with either.[20]

The Casa emerged at a time when workers in Mexico City had begun organizing with increasing assertiveness, given the political opening under Madero. Madero had pleaded with the emergent unions to show restraint when it came to strikes and demonstrations, and to await what he referred to as "administrative progress."[21] Workers' confidence continued to grow, however, and in 1912 the Casa successfully called the first May Day march in Mexican history. Even after Madero's fall its work continued, including a march presenting demands for an eight-hour day and a six-day week to the Huertista Congress. The Casa focused on the economic struggle rather than joining the armed revolt, and Huerta allowed it to operate legally for most of his rule.

But it was in the months after Huerta's defeat that the ranks of the Casa grew significantly, as workers increasingly joined unions, and these affiliated with the new federation. By the time of the split at the Aguascalientes Convention, the Casa claimed fifty-two thousand members in twenty-three affiliated unions. The numbers may have been somewhat exaggerated, but the change was significant. It was no longer a group of only skilled workers, but also had a large component of industrial and unskilled labor. When Carranza first arrived in the capital prior to his defeat at the Convention, the Casa presented to him its demands for labor reform, which Obregón later seized upon to radicalize the Constitutionalist program.

Later, upon retaking Mexico City in 1915, Obregón went to the Casa almost immediately. He ordered the confiscation of a wealthy convent, along with the printing press belonging to an influential Catholic newspaper; both were given to the Casa for its own use. The choice of the convent was deliberately symbolic: it was a site where members of Porfirian high society often chose to marry. Later the Jockey Club—another long-standing institution of the Porfirian elite—was confiscated and given to the Casa as well. The Casa was also provided with cash to distribute directly to its unemployed members. But Obregón went even further than this, intervening directly to assist labor struggles. One important ongoing conflict, for example, was of electricians and operators with the Mexican Telephone and Telegraph Company. The Convention had been unable to resolve the strike during its rule in the capital. Obregón, by contrast, simply expropriated the company and put the union in charge of its management. A young trade unionist named Luis Morones was made the boss of the enterprise, and all the strikebreakers were fired.* Such measures were both popular and impressive among workers. One Zapatista general highlighted this key difference between the camps, noting that "the enemy is growing, winning the sympathies of the People, on account of our apathy."[22]

So what did Obregón want? Ultimately not just popularity, but military support. His agitators were relentless in trade union and worker meetings. Obregón and his allies were making considerable progress in painting Villa as a "reactionary," given some of the unsavory characters—hacendados, prominent churchmen, former Federal Army officers—in his forces. They also pointed to Obregón's radical proworker measures, as against the weak record of the Convention. And so in February 1915, at a meeting of sixty-seven leaders of the Casa, after much debate it was decided to offer support to the Constitutionalists. Later, a general meeting of three thousand workers ended without a clear agreement. The organization was divided, but the pro-Obregón elements in the Casa leadership went forward. They cemented the alliance and formed volunteer "Red Battalions," composed of workers, to join the Constitutionalists in the fight against Villa. Some five to seven thousand workers, a significant number, eventually signed up.[23]

So how did this happen? What of the anarchist influence in the Casa, for example? Some might argue that the workers were just

---

* He would later become one of the postrevolutionary regime's most notoriously corrupt labor supporters, the first of the so-called *charro*, or cowboy, union leaders.

deceived, or outmaneuvered. But this is far too simple: for many workers and their leaders there was something compelling about Obregón's arguments, in comparison to the more anarchist ideas in play in the labor movement. For the pro-Obregón Casa leaders, the Constitutionalists' policies offered the best chance to expand labor's reach in various parts of the country where it had previously held little influence. Some also saw the pact as a gamble of sorts: they knew it wouldn't last forever, but it could put them in a much stronger and more influential position when the civil war was over. The Casa was growing by leaps and bounds, and it wanted to seize the opportunity. And this it did, aggressively organizing unions in cities as they fell to the Constitutionalists, much to Carranza's annoyance.

The longer-standing Casa leaders had certainly stood firm in the past against any involvement in politics. Yet the anarchist-influenced arguments that placed a wall between workplace organizing and political action were ultimately unconvincing to many urban workers in the Casa, and beyond.[24] A number of new leaders who had recently entered the organization were also unconvinced. There had been a tremendous growth in political engagement among workers since the time Díaz's regime had begun to falter; this had continued during the Revolution, despite workers' disappointments with Madero.[25] Trade unionists were now faced with a major civil war in Mexico, and they became convinced that they should ensure that its outcome was favorable to them. That labor should remain neutral, or that all sides should lay down their arms—the principal counterargument to Obregón—fell short.

Yet why not ally with Zapata and his campesino forces instead? Certainly the proverbial "game plan" of twentieth-century revolutionary doctrine was for the urban proletariat to ally with the rural peasantry. Some scholars of the Revolution have argued (with the benefit of hindsight, of course) that such an alliance might have led the Revolution to carry out far more radical changes.[26] From this perspective, the responsibility for promoting such a strategy would fall to the ostensibly most radical figures in this period—that is, those identified with anarchism.

Yet their opposition to political engagement was again a key factor. According to historian John Lear, when it came to the conflict between the Villa-Zapata forces and those of Carranza-Obregón, there were Casa leaders who "prided themselves in their neutrality in what they still perceived largely as a political struggle." Indeed, one leading Casa member had been expelled from the organization for participating in the Aguascalientes Convention as a Zapatista delegate. Earlier, the Casa leadership had also remained silent during the Decena Trágica (the Huerta coup against Madero) and in the weeks following.[27] Such positions undoubtedly frustrated many workers interested in and concerned with political affairs.

There is another possible reason that many radical Casa leaders kept their distance from the Zapatistas: the former were highly anticlerical, and interested in propagating secular and rationalist ideas among the working class. They believed that this sort of thoroughgoing education was essential for workers to be able to change society. This outlook thus made some Casa leaders sympathetic to Obregón, who was clearly hostile to the Church. Obregón had already confiscated religious property, demanded Church funds, and even attempted to forcibly enlist the priests of the capital into his armies—later revealing to the public that some forty-nine of them had to be rejected due to their having venereal disease.[28]

The Zapatista campesinos, in contrast, marched into Mexico City behind banners of the widely revered Virgin of Guadalupe. To be sure, the Zapatistas had also supported measures directed against the Church, such as the establishment of universal state-sponsored secular education. Nonetheless, the stereotype of the superstitious campesino, in thrall to the priest and pulpit, was difficult to shake among many anticlerical radicals. Indeed, Obregón made this part of his propaganda against Zapata and his followers. Moreover, there were Casa leaders who later helped to further this stereotype once they were allied with Obregón.

Strong anticlerical feelings could also be found among workers and the poor in Mexico City.[29] After all, the Church hierarchy had clearly backed the dictator Huerta, and was seen by many as a servant of the elite. Yet poor Mexicans could be hostile to the Church, or the local priest, and still keep a shrine to the Virgin in their home. It is unlikely that the Zapatistas' religious symbols or beliefs were a significant obstacle in forming alliances. By all accounts their relations with workers and the poor in Mexico City were cordial. A more important factor was that as far as the Zapatistas were concerned, an alliance with urban workers wasn't a priority: they did not need urban streetcar conductors or printers or electricians in their forces in order to take back their lands in Morelos.

In assessing the Casa's decisions, one should also consider the historical moment, and the steps taken without the benefit of hindsight. Many radicals internationally, of various stripes, had not arrived at the conclusion that a progressive urban social class—the working class—should ally with and make concessions to a "backward" and "precapitalist" class like the peasantry. It was not part of the vision of progress many revolutionaries held. The classic alliance of the proletariat and peasantry had not yet been given the impetus that derived from Russia's Bolshevik Revolution of October 1917. Other anarchist-influenced radicals (like Antonio Díaz Soto y Gama and Manuel Palafox) did ally with the campesinos, but they did so by joining Zapata's movement and moving to the countryside of Morelos. They largely focused their efforts there, hoping to build a rural agrarian socialism, rather than building explicit alliances with the working class.

Another question sometimes raised is whether the alliance with labor made a difference in the Revolution and to Obregón's victory. Historians rightly point out that the Red Batallions were composed of relatively raw recruits and thus may not have been a major military factor.[30] But this approach fails to look at the question in political terms: what if workers and their unions had cemented an alliance with the other side, with Villa and Zapata? It would have dealt a serious blow to Obregón's efforts, and he knew this. At minimum, it might have been difficult for him to maintain his military rear guard and his supply lines while he challenged Villa. But even more important, Obregón's plans for national control would have proved a difficult proposition if he had faced the active (if not armed) opposition of the working class of the capital.

None of this, however, was to be. With his working-class reinforcements, Obregón marched out to face Villa on the north-central plains of the Mexican Bajío in the spring of 1915.

The Constitutionalists Prevail over Villa

The showdown between Villa and Obregón—undoubtedly Mexico's two best generals—had been expected since the bitter split at the Convention the previous year. Obregón made the first move against Villa, but he was deliberate: his troops advanced carefully, maintaining their supply lines through Mexico City and Puebla to the Constitutionalist headquarters on the coast in Veracruz.

Harassing Obregón's rear and interrupting his supply lines were the Zapatistas' responsibility. But they failed to do this, much to Villa's frustration. The crucial city of Puebla, a gateway to Mexico City, had been allowed to fall to the Constitutionalists, in large part due to military and political sloppiness.[31] Indeed, the military strategy of the Villa-Zapata alliance—dictated in part by provincial concerns—resulted in an "absurd dispersal of forces," according to one enemy general, which allowed for a "miraculous salvation of the Constitutionalist side."[32]

This dispersal reflected the Zapatista troops' loss of interest in far-flung campaigns with seemingly distant goals. Their focus was back on Morelos: they were busy carrying out a social revolution in their domains. The remaining hacienda lands in the state were distributed to local villages. The region's sugar mills were collectivized and placed under Zapatista control. Zapata's public declarations became more and more radical, in part under the influence of the left-wing intellectuals in his camp: he now spoke of the goal of socialism in Morelos. Later he even began to issue appeals to the urban working class, but it was in many respects too late.

Zapata was nonetheless carrying out the dream he had fought for. He spent much of his time administering the process of land distribution and resolving village conflicts. He tried to convince the campesinos to grow sugar for sale, rather than solely subsistence crops, to help develop the region. But he also spent his time hanging out drinking in village squares, betting on cock-fights, attending (and performing in) rodeos, and apparently having multiple romantic affairs. For the moment, life seemed to be peaceful and relatively prosperous in Morelos.

But this was possible only because the attention of the Zapatistas' enemies was focused elsewhere. Beyond Morelos, the war was being joined against Villa. Obregón's forces were still outnumbered, but his strategy was based on one key thing he knew about

Woodcut image of Zapata

his rival: Villa could not resist the challenge of a straight-up fight. Villa's military advisers—including the savvy Felipe Ángeles—counseled patience. The key was to harass Obregón forces, and allow him to extend himself farther and farther into the north seeking out Villa's army. It was better, they argued, to wait and fight on your own terms, rather than on your enemy's. But Villa would have none of it. He later recalled, "If I fell back before Obregón, or clung to what's called the defensive, the prestige of my troops and my own reputation would suffer in the eyes of the enemy. After all, when . . . have we let the enemy tire himself out looking for us in our territory?

When have I not gone out to fight him, shattering him with my momentum, putting him to rout?"[33] Villa was, if anything, consistent in his military strategy. But it made him predictable. Moreover, he underestimated Obregón, a man he often called *el perfumado*—the perfumed one—in trying to frame him as a soft urbanite. In reality Obregón would prove to be the most formidable opponent Villa would ever face.

The opposing troops battled over the course of three months near the towns Celaya and León, in the north-central state of Guanajuato. But one day Obregón's plans—or at least his part in them—were almost destroyed by chance. Overlooking the scene of an upcoming battle with his general staff, he was surprised by a sudden Villista artillery attack. The men fled to the trenches, but a shell exploded near Obregón, blowing off his right arm. He was quickly losing blood, and believed himself to be done for. Obregón drew his service revolver and put it to his temple, to give himself the final coup de grace. He pulled the trigger—and his gun said: *Click*. And again: *Click*. In one of those chance events on which history turns, Obregón's assistant had forgotten to reload his pistol after cleaning it the night before. Obregón was rescued, and his wound was successfully treated. The famous arm, years later, would end up preserved in a monument to the general in Mexico City.

Obregón henceforth led his troops with one arm, and in several hard-fought and bloody battles his forces ultimately routed the legendary Northern Division. Villa's repeated furious frontal attacks often came close to succeeding, but they were repulsed by Obregón's well-entrenched troops and then decimated by his astute counterattacks. Villa was now in full retreat, his men deserting, and towns in Chihuahua began falling to the Constitutionalists. After regrouping his remaining forces, Villa attempted to open another front by attacking at the town of Agua Prieta in neighboring Sonora. This also ended in defeat, in large part because the town had been secretly reinforced by troops passing though the United States. Following Villa's military setbacks, Washington had finally elected, reluctantly, to endorse Carranza.[34]

Villa soon experienced a crucial problem of caudillo-style leadership: what had united his forces was Villa himself, more than a clear set of shared ideals. When his strength turned to weakness, when the caudillo failed in battle, when he could no longer provide for "his people," many of them would desert him. Obregón offered Villa amnesty for his remaining men, and even exile in the United States. At this point it was clear to all that Villa had been beaten— except to Villa. Refusing to surrender, he returned to the place where he began: guerrilla warfare. He was no longer the great patron of Chihuahua, but with a much-reduced band of hard-core loyalists he continued to fight.

Villa's increasingly isolated forces began a process of hit-and-run warfare, conducting successful lightning raids throughout Chihuahua in the subsequent years. At one point Villa spent weeks hiding in a remote cave, recovering from an infected wound, but he was still too proud to give in to his enemies. He continued to denounce Carranza, but more and more it seemed as if his forces were merely lashing out, seeking revenge, and lacking a clear or consistent political objective. While power never seemed to have entirely corrupted Villa, his growing powerlessness perhaps did. Violence and cruelty, more than social or political goals, came to be his fighters' most notable quality.

Such was the case in a gruesome incident in Santa Rosalía, Chihuahua, in December 1916. Following the capture of a train hub that had been in Constitutionalist hands, some ninety soldaderas, their men now dead or wounded, were assembled and awaiting their fate. Villa had always disdained the soldaderas in the old Northern Division—believing them to limit the mobility and discipline of his troops—but he had never been able to get rid of them due to opposition among his soldiers. Now, while Villa was passing the assembled women in Santa Rosalía, a gunshot was fired from among them, striking his sombrero. Villa immediately demanded that the would-be assassin be handed over. The women steadfastly refused. As punishment, Villa had all ninety of them executed on the spot.

Another incident in April 1917 made clear how brutal Villa's methods had become, and how isolated he was from the people who had once given him support. Certain residents of the village of Namiquipa, who were sympathetic to Carranza, had betrayed the location of one of Villa's secret munitions depots. Following a particularly bitter military defeat, Villa decided to take his revenge. His troops marched to Namiquipa, and upon their arrival, the armed Carrancista loyalists fled into the mountains, leaving the women behind. Villa ordered his men to gather up all the women of the town and rape them. Several of his commanders refused to comply with this order, and sheltered as many women as they could. The news of this horrific attack spread far and wide, and helped to severely undermine Villa's standing among the people of the region.[35]

Villa had also developed a visceral hostility toward the United States following the defeat of the Northern Division. After being a clear focus of American attentions—including a Hollywood movie—Villa had been cast aside as the United States decided to support Carranza. Americans thus became a target. Around this time, one of Villa's generals captured a team of seventeen US mining engineers working in the north, and summarily executed them all. Villa even conducted a raid into New Mexico, killing a number of Americans and finally provoking a hapless US expedition in pursuit of him. This move was not as crazy as it seemed: it led to an embargo of weapons to Mexico and ensured that Carranza could not obtain arms and loans from the United States. Villa was, at minimum, an interminable pest for the new government. Moreover, as a guerrilla, he was nearly impossible to capture or kill.

Carranza in Power and the Jacobin Response

The defeat of the Northern Division had another significant outcome: Carranza's path to power was finally clear. He returned to Mexico City in August 1915 and assumed the presidency. At this point conditions in many parts of the country were dire. The nation was devastated and exhausted from years of warfare. Food was scarce and costly, as the disruptions occasioned by civil war had made planting and harvesting impossible in many regions. Various diseases were spreading, and were killing people in large numbers, particularly in the cities. In Mexico City, trees in the elegant Porfirian parks were being chopped down for fuel. Inflation was rampant: both factions had produced their own paper currency, and it was now nearly worthless. The railroad lines were in a state of disarray, where not destroyed. The breakdown in political authority in many regions led to widespread banditry, but now it wasn't directed against the haciendas and the rich but against the terrified residents of villages and towns.

In this context, the Constitutionalist military was now the most powerful institution in the country, and its officer corps the most influential group on a national level. Carranza had to maintain a delicate balance with them. On the one hand, although he wished to carry out an unvarnished pro-landlord agenda, his efforts were often checked by his young Jacobin officers, who still advocated substantial reform. These included people like Francisco Múgica and Salvador Alvarado, the generals who took the Revolution to the nation's south. Obregón was also a part of this camp.

On the other hand, Carranza also had to conciliate those Constitutionalist generals who weren't especially interested in social reform. With the old Porfirian elite booted from power, these men wanted no government interference in their backyards, and attempted to monopolize local political power. Reforms might be granted, but only if in line with their own priorities. Frequently their goal was to simply enrich themselves and their allies. According to Alvarado, Carranza was surrounded by such "servile sycophants hoping to line their pockets with money."[36] One case was the Constitutionalist general Alfredo Ricault, who in exchange for his continued loyalty requested "a Cadillac automobile, vintage 1916," in a letter to Carranza. For good measure, Ricault pointed out that car was "one of those you gave to General Luis Caballero."[37]

Carranza knew he had to first appease the radicals to some extent. He thus called a constitutional convention to replace Mexico's former charter of 1857. The Jacobin reformers, hoping to define the framework of the postrevolutionary regime, eagerly took up the challenge of writing a new founding political document for

Mexico. The delegates who met in the city of Querétaro in December 1916 were overwhelmingly educated men of the middle class. There would be no agrarian appeals from Zapatista representatives as there had been at the Convention only two years before. Nonetheless, the document the delegates produced—against numerous objections from Carranza—strongly reflected the previous years of popular revolt. The radical wing at the Constitutional Convention was led by Múgica. While Carranza's original draft had been a cautious reformulation of the 1857 charter, the revised version, when completed in January 1917, was likely the most radical constitution in the world of its time. Article 123 enshrined the rights to join unions and to strike, established the eight-hour workday and a minimum wage, and stipulated a range of social welfare provisions. The famed Article 27—a lengthy and detailed tract on its own—made expropriation of land by the state legal, nullified the alienations of village land carried out under the Porfirian regime, and mandated the creation and protection of small-scale and communal landownership. Also included were far-reaching measures in education and limiting the power of the Catholic Church.

But words were one thing and implementation another. The cruel irony was that in spite of Article 27, and his own previous declarations on agrarian reform, Carranza dug in his heels. From 1915 to 1920, a mere 173,000 hectares of land were distributed to forty-four thousand campesinos.[38] Recall that an area roughly the size of California had been privatized under the Porfiriato; thus only 0.4 percent of this land was officially recovered during Carranza's presidency. Múgica went so far as to describe the situation under Carranza as a "complete fiasco."[39] Moreover, Carranza was also actively attempting to return confiscated properties to the landlords. To this end, all lands that had been seized or nationalized during the conflict were centralized in an office within the executive branch, under Carranza's direct control. The final decisions effectively rested with him, and his policy from 1916 to 1919 was to return the estates whenever possible. In San Luis Potosí alone, for example, 240 houses and 72 haciendas were returned to their original owners, a sign of both Carranza's zeal for returning property and the extent of the original expropriations.[40] In Chihuahua, plans were even set in motion to sell Luis Terrazas's vast estates to an American investor, backed by a major Wall Street bank.

When Carranza did grant or lease confiscated property to other parties, it was not to campesinos but to many of his own military officers, in order to secure their loyalty. Indeed, a number of Constitutionalist generals—typically those less reform-minded—soon became big landowners in various parts of Mexico.[41] Shortly before his death in 1919, Zapata wrote an angry open letter to Carranza describing this process: "In agrarian matters, the haciendas have been granted or leased to your favorite generals; the old estates of the high bourgeoisie, in more than a few cases, are taken over by modern landowners who boast [military] epaulettes, a helmet, and a pistol in their belt."[42] There were other army officers who went into business and commerce, in initiatives ranging from gambling houses to construction firms; the latter benefited greatly from government reconstruction contracts after the armed conflict was over. In short, they seized the opportunities created by the dislocation and instability of the Revolution, especially given the retreat of the old Porfirian elite. There were also military leaders who gained wealth through more parasitic means; these men would become legendary for their avarice and corruption. Some enriched themselves through control of transit routes, particularly the railroads; others offered themselves as "protection" for landlords, defending them against expropriation; others engaged in various forms of extortion; still others just robbed unfortunate villages at gunpoint. Motivated mainly by personal ambition rather than reformist ideals, these individuals sought to finally obtain what they believed was theirs, as the rich had so easily done before.

Meanwhile, Carranza went on the offensive against the labor movement. This included breaking the former alliance with the Casa del Obrero Mundial; the unions that had supported Carranza's camp would soon be in direct conflict with the First Chief. Although his government was still weak, it had aspirations to establish itself as an advocate for the nation's battered landlords and wealthy businessmen. The Red Batallions were disbanded, and the Casa was evicted from the Jockey Club. A Mexico City general strike declared in the summer of 1916—demanding that workers be paid in gold rather than paper currency—was put down by force. "The destruction of the tyranny of capitalism," Carranza declared, could not be followed by "the tyranny of the workers."[43] He went so far as to decree the death penalty for going on strike; the decree, in part, read as follows:

> The death penalty shall be applied ... to those who incite or spread a work stoppage in factories or other enterprises designed to maintain public services; who chair meetings in which such a stoppage is proposed, discussed or approved; who advocate and support such a stoppage; who attend a meeting of this kind and fail to withdraw as soon as they realize its purpose; or who try to make a stoppage effective as soon as it has been declared.[44]

Pressure from the labor movement and the Jacobin elements in the military prevented such sentences from being carried out. Nonetheless, repression forced the Casa out of existence.

Carranza did not stop there: with Villa effectively out of the picture, the defeat of radical campesino movements across Mexico now became his principal military objective. A number of prominent agrarian leaders were eventually defeated or killed by Carranza's forces. Of those mentioned previously, Calixto Contreras was killed in the Laguna, in June 1916; Alberto Carrera Torres in Tamaulipas, in February 1917; Domingo Arenas in Tlaxcala, in August 1917; and Jesús Salgado in Guerrero, in June 1919. But the subjugation of Morelos was the most important—and challenging—goal of all. The years from 1916 onward would be cruel and difficult for the campesinos of the region. The armies of the new government carried out multiple scorched-earth campaigns in the state, much as Madero and Huerta had done before. The Zapatista rebels were chased into the hills, while entire villages were put to the torch and their residents expelled. In 1918 alone, the population of Morelos declined by a quarter due to emigration, disease, and warfare.

While they could not be fully crushed, Zapata and his forces became increasingly isolated and desperate. The movement began to unravel internally; some of its leaders and allies even elected to defect and accept amnesty from the authorities. Others began to raid the villages in order to maintain their troops, much to Zapata's anger and disgust. Various officers were shot for corruption and conciliating the enemy. Meanwhile, Zapata's brother—who had always been a bit too authoritarian with his men—was killed in a drunken brawl with one of his officers, who promptly fled and took his troops to join the Constitutionalists. Manuel Palafox, the radical young intellectual, also was cast out. He was secretly attracted to men and had begun making sexual advances toward the officers at Zapatista headquarters. Zapata—consistent with the antihomosexual attitudes of his day—was furious, and wanted Palafox shot. In the end he was exiled, and also joined the enemy.

Although weakened, Zapata could ultimately be eliminated only by treachery. In order to survive, the Zapatista movement had begun reaching out to unlikely allies, even ones who did not share their program. The Plan de Ayala was quietly shelved for more moderate appeals. One potential supporter, it seemed, was the Constitutionalist colonel Jesús Guajardo. Once he had systematically butchered the residents of a Zapatista village who refused to pay taxes to the national government. Now, he claimed, he wished to defect to the side of the Morelos rebels with his men. It was perhaps a sign of Zapata's increasing desperation that he even took him seriously. To prove his credibility, Guajardo declared himself in revolt, and went so far as to execute fifty-nine of his own men. Zapata was convinced, and decided to meet with him in April 1919. At their first meeting, Zapata was given a gift of a fine horse. The following day, Zapata arrived at Guajardo's camp with a small escort. Guajardo's soldiers, pretending to greet Zapata with an armed salute, instead opened fire on him. Zapata was killed instantly. Although the assassination was never directly linked to orders from Carranza, Guajardo was given a generous financial reward by the First Chief—fifty thousand pesos in gold—along with a promotion to general. The agrarian struggle in Morelos and beyond would have to try to continue without its greatest figure.

And yet continue it did. Agrarian movements, including Zapata's, could survive military defeats, and even the death of their leaders. They had faced severe repression before. As their villages burned, in some cases the women also began to fight. According to historian John Womack, in Puente de Ixtla, Morelos, "the wives, daughters, and sisters of rebels formed their own battalion and revolted to 'avenge the dead.' Under the command of a husky extortilla maker called La China, they raided wildly through Tetecala district. Some in rags, some in plundered finery, wearing silk stockings and dresses, sandals, straw hats, and gun belts, these women became the terrors of the region." Even Zapatista general Genovevo de la O, a very tough customer in his own right, reportedly "treated La China with respect."[45]

And so the campesinos of Morelos, time and again, refused to give in. Moreover, there were other independent agrarian rebellions or movements, large and small, which could not be eliminated by Carranza's campaigns. Among them were the rebels in San Luis Potosí: they were now led by Saturnino Cedillo, alone, since all of his brothers were dead. Cedillo still commanded as many as three thousand fighters, but according to one observer these were "bearded, long-haired, half-naked men."[46] The armed campesino loyalists of the late Domingo Arenas in Tlaxcala also continued to press their claims to land, and the Constitutionalist governor feared them enough to avoid touching the land they had already taken, despite Carranza's orders. On the gulf coast, in Veracruz, militant labor and agrarian movements were on the rise, leading to a state of constant ferment that would continue through the 1920s. Farther north, in Sonora, the Yaqui people had started a revolt to recover their ancestral lands, and could not be put down despite repeated bloody military campaigns. In short, Carranza couldn't achieve his counterrevolution everywhere, and the corrupt

Constitutionalist nouveaux-riches didn't always have their way. Alan Knight has rightly summarized Carranza's challenge as that of "grappling with an inflated balloon: pressure at one point (like Morelos) was redistributed elsewhere, thus creating new excrescences which had to be contained."[47]

Most significantly, Carranza's attempts to reverse the course of the Revolution were not only repellent to many workers and campesinos. They were also unwelcome among the Jacobin wing of the military, including its most prominent representative, Álvaro Obregón. These figures believed that the radical new Constitution of 1917 should not be simply a dead letter; indeed, some of them had helped write it. In their view, campesino and worker rebellion had to be dealt with via managed reform, not further warfare.

It was increasingly clear that while Carranza was able to weaken the popular forces that made his presidency possible, he was never ever able to fully subdue them. After years of upheaval, his refusal to make concessions to the lower classes, and his attempts to reestablish the power of the old landlords, made it difficult for him to consolidate the state's authority. Villa in the north, Zapata's movement in the south, the trade unions, campesino radicals in pockets around the country—they simply would not go away. While they could not win, they stubbornly refused to be defeated.[48] It was an unstable, even untenable, situation.

Salvador Alvarado's maxim in favor of social reform should be remembered here: "Give them land, and you bind them to Mexico"— not as enemies, but as subordinate participants within the political regime. This sort of arrangement could best guarantee social harmony, stability, and the growth of a capitalist economy in Mexico after nearly a decade of war. The strategy of the postrevolutionary system had already begun to take shape, in both the minds and the practice of the Jacobin military officers. Even the more conservative elements in the army, and among former military men, feared a loss of their newfound power and property ownership with the efforts to restore the position of the old landlords. And so these military officers—the main organized power on a national level—would eventually turn on Carranza. They would also form a powerful core of the postrevolutionary establishment.

Obregón, meanwhile, had since left his position under Carranza as minister of war and was spending his time in civilian life building a commercial chickpea empire in Sonora. But in 1919 he declared his intention to run for president in the 1920 elections. The goal was to right the revolutionary ship and move away from Carranza's nakedly pro-landlord political approach. Obregón's campaign for the presidency quickly sought to incorporate all the dissenting factions among campesinos, workers, and military officers. The Zapatistas, under Zapata's successor, gave him their backing; later their intellectual leader Antonio Díaz Soto y Gama would found the Agrarian Party, an important pillar of support for the Obregón government. Luis Morones, the electrician's union leader, backed Obregón as well, along with his new labor federation, which was established after the defeat of the Casa. Morones also founded the Labor Party, which would become another pillar of the future regime. Obregón was rebuilding the radical Jacobin coalitions of 1915, but in a context where the forces of workers and campesinos were considerably weaker and more conciliatory.

Carranza, however, would not support his former general and his campaign, which threatened his vision of how Mexico should be governed. He declared his support instead for a pro-landlord crony, who would continue his agenda. To further interrupt Obregón's candidacy, Carranza's government eventually brought treason charges against him. In response, Obregón and his supporters called for revolt. The entire armed forces quickly came over to Obregón's side. Carranza was nearly alone: despite his attempts to revive the landowners' political and economic fortunes, the rich still had no forces in Mexico that would fight for them and their representatives. The new army was clearly not with them.

As military rebellion swept the country, Carranza fled the capital in May 1920, with the contents of the national treasury in tow. He once again headed for Veracruz. This time he never made it. In a final moment of historical irony, Carranza's train was attacked by none other than Jesús Guajuardo, Zapata's assassin. General Guajardo—undoubtedly one of the Revolution's great opportunists—had decided to come over to Obregón's side.* Forced to flee into the mountains, Carranza met up with troops he believed to be loyal. He was mistaken, however, and they killed him in the village of Tlaxcalontongo while he slept. Elections were held later that year, and Obregón assumed power on December 1, 1920.

The final rebel holdout was Pancho Villa. He had continued to fight, briefly seizing villages and towns across the north. The post-Carranza caretaker government decided to make an offer of peace to Villa, via emissaries. Villa countered with an offer to lay down his arms in exchange for amnesty for himself and his men. But he also demanded: a large ranch in Durango (he had already picked it out); a personal bodyguard of 50 men, their salaries paid

---

* Following another shift in loyalties, Guajardo was finally captured and executed later that same year.

for by the government; land and cash for his remaining 750 or so loyal soldiers; and that his rank of general be officially recognized. Obregón's representatives told him to take a hike. And so he did. Villa saved his most remarkable feat for last: he decided on another surprise attack, but to do so required crossing the Mapimi Bulge. The idea was utter madness: then, as now, the Mapimi was a vast, merciless expanse of bone-dry desert, stretching southward from west Texas. No one had ever done it before; probably no one had even tried it before. Yet Villa, somehow, did. He and his men left Saucillo, Chihuahua, on horseback, arriving a grueling five days later at Sabinas, Coahuila—and successfully attacked the garrison there. Villa then cabled the government, informing them of his location, and reiterated his demands. At first the officials thought the man had finally lost his marbles. Soon they realized their error. They agreed to his demands.

Conclusion

With Villa, the last of the Revolution's powerful armed leaders had made his peace with the new regime. He had given in, but he had never surrendered, and he had some say in the terms. The same might be said of the labor and campesino forces during the Revolution. Moreover, even after the Revolution was officially over they continued to fight and press their demands across Mexico.

The historian Adolfo Gilly has described the events of 1910–20 as a revolution that was "interrupted."[49] How might we interpret this? On the one hand, Gilly means that certain higher goals that the most radical elements in the Revolution aspired to—thoroughgoing land reform, for example, or even some form of anticapitalism—were not achieved. But it also means that after the dust settled, no organized social group was in a position to exercise a dominant influence over the postrevolutionary state. Landlords and capitalists, urban workers, and campesinos were all weakened—battered and exhausted—by ten years of social conflict, deprivation, and bloody warfare. Thus by 1920, the state had acquired an exceptional degree of power relative to the rest of society. It was largely directed by a new military caste; indeed, in the fifteen years following the Revolution, military officers held roughly half of the state governorships in Mexico (a still influential position), as well as a disproportionate number of posts in the upper echelons of government.[50] Many of them were social reformers, and many of them were nouveau-riches, or aspiring to it. A good number were both. The model figure of the age was the general-turned-politician-turned-businessman or some variant thereof. Such opportunities made them loyal to the regime; as Obregón famously put it, "no general can withstand a cannon-shot of 50,000 pesos."[51]

The new rulers' goal was to advance Mexico's economy through capitalist economic development—often with themselves as the capitalists—while avoiding social conflict. Salvador Alvarado, the Constitutionalist military officer and social reformer, believed—as did many of his peers—that "the state has the solution in its hands." The state, by making concessions to the campesino and worker when necessary, would ensure peace and stability so that "the capitalist could dedicate himself to his business, without the present anxieties that mar his work." In other words, it was necessary to ensure that popular revolt be a thing of the past. Alvarado would also affirm that "under my government [in Yucatán] no farmworker would ever raise a hand against a landowner."[52]

This perspective was often proclaimed with radical language, and the new leaders often identified this state-supervised capitalism as a form of socialism. This was not seen as the victory of labor over capital, or campesino over landlord, but rather a careful balance between the different sides. As Obregón put it, "Socialism has as its principal vision extending a hand to those at the bottom [of society], in order to seek a better equilibrium between capital and labor."[53]

The leaders who held to this postrevolutionary vision also believed that the dominant position of the state had to be respected by all its subjects. Those who made appeals or demands to the new political regime but remained loyal to it, and were willing to negotiate and concede, were often rewarded. Those who attempted to work outside the system, or question its legitimacy, often faced the use of force. One notable case was the Yaqui people of Sonora, many of whom had marched with Obregón in the years before 1920. They had continued to fight for a promised agrarian reform after the Revolution was declared to be over, and in the new president's own backyard no less. The people who had once been Obregón's valiant bowmen were now seen as little more than troublesome Indians. They were finally put down with the use of military aircraft.

Another more symbolic case was the assassination of Pancho Villa. He was finally killed in 1923, gunned down along with four members of his guard while driving his 1919 Dodge Roadster through the streets of Parral, Chihuahua. The killing was very likely on Obregón's orders. The president seems to have feared that Villa was planning to get involved in yet another antigovernment uprising, something he had in fact been threatening to do.

These sorts of examples might indicate the end of an era—that the spirit of revolt that marked the years from 1910 to 1920 was finished. Yet that would be mistaken. It would also be mistaken to assume that campesino organizations and labor unions could approach the state only on bended knee. They maintained a measure of independence and combativeness under the postrevolutionary regime. To take one example, there were 310 "legal" strikes—meaning by labor organizations approved by the regime—in 1921 alone, involving more than 100,000 workers.[54] More of the population, especially among the lower social classes, was mobilized and participating in politics than anywhere else in Latin America at this time.[55]

Moreover, the new state was still unsteady, and depended on support from campesinos and labor. It was thus often willing to make concessions, while trying to bring the various popular organizations sprouting up across the country under its control. Those regions where campesinos had been the most rebellious, and had tenaciously maintained their organizations, were the earliest and most consistent recipients of land reform. In Morelos, for example, 115 of the state's 150 villages received new land titles under the first postrevolutionary regime; in neighboring Puebla, there were 138 land grants, and in the radical hotbed of Veracruz there were 129.[56] Yet even in these places—as well as elsewhere in Mexico where the government was less generous—campesino struggle (and even armed conflict) did not disappear after 1920.

These persistent popular organizations would play a major role during the presidency of Lázaro Cárdenas (1934–40), Mexico's greatest postrevolutionary social reformer. He turned to workers and campesinos for support, and finally carried out a wholesale expropriation of hacienda land once and for all in Mexico. More than twenty-five million hectares of land were distributed, more than had been undertaken by all his predecessors combined. It was the largest land reform in Latin American history. Cárdenas also decreed the nationalization of the oil industry, against stiff opposition from the United States. These reforms were immensely popular, and it was through such measures that his presidency would ultimately cement the alliance between the state and various campesino and labor organizations.

Following World War II, however, the Mexican government and its new authoritarian ruling party, the Party of the Institutionalized Revolution (PRI), assumed a more conservative and probusiness posture. Mexico's economy was booming once again. At the same time, the fruits of the postrevolutionary political arrangement had led to popular organizations that were in an increasingly subordinate position vis-à-vis the PRI. Their job was to support the ruling party, get out the vote in elections, perhaps help stuff ballot boxes, or perhaps intimidate opposition voters at polling stations. Many of these popular organizations would not break from this role, given that loyalty seemed like the best way to obtain rewards for their members, and given that their leaders increasingly benefited from government patronage and corruption. A carrot-and-stick approach, meaning selective concessions and the selective use of violence, was employed by PRI governments with great skill. Those who loyally remained within the PRI's circle might hope to receive the carrot; those outside were increasingly marginalized. Moreover, when social reform went radically in the other direction beginning in the 1980s—directed by the PRI itself—these same organizations had little capability to mobilize and organize independently of the regime. They had become, in many cases, empty shells, and were limited in the extent they could challenge the new neoliberal reforms. It is this more recent reform era, begun a generation ago, that has greatly shaped the Mexico of today.

This is only a brief summary of a long and tortuous history since the events of 1910–20. As mentioned at the start, this short book cannot hope to untangle the Revolution's complex legacy. But one important goal here—as is always the case with the study of history—is that understanding the human conflicts of the past can provide a means to better understand our world in the present.

Timeline of Major Events

February 1908: Aging dictator Porfirio Díaz gives the widely discussed "Creelman interview," where he speaks of his openness to an opposition presidential candidate in Mexico.

September 1909: Emiliano Zapata is elected village president of Anenecuilco, Morelos. Campesinos led by Zapata begin repossessing land from the local sugar haciendas.

April 1910: Francisco Madero officially launches an opposition presidential campaign, gaining widespread support.

June 1910: Madero is jailed by the Díaz regime, for "attempts at rebellion and insults to the authorities."

July 1910: Díaz is dubiously "elected" president for the eighth time.

October 1910: Madero escapes from jail and issues his call to revolt, the Plan de San Luis Potosí. The Plan calls for political democracy in Mexico, and vaguely states that agrarian questions would be "subject to review" in a post-Díaz government.

November 1910–May 1911: Madero's revolt begins slowly and then gathers steam, especially in the Mexican north. Pancho Villa, a former bandit, joins the rebellion against Díaz in Chihuahua. In Morelos, Zapata's forces do battle with Díaz's Federal Army.

May 1911: Following numerous defeats at the hands of the rebels, Díaz resigns the presidency and leaves for exile in Europe.

October 1911: Madero is elected president of Mexico.

November 1911: Zapata and his followers break publicly with Madero, and accuse him of betraying the agrarian cause. They issue the Plan de Ayala, calling for radical agrarian reform in Mexico. Madero orders the Federal Army to put down the Zapatista rebellion.

May 1912: General Victoriano Huerta, a conservative Porfirian-era general, has Pancho Villa arrested on charges of stealing a horse. Villa has remained a loyal supporter of Madero and is already a popular militia leader in Chihuahua. Villa barely avoids execution and is instead jailed in Mexico City.

December 1912: Villa escapes from prison in Mexico City and flees to Texas.

February 1913: General Huerta overthrows Madero during the "Tragic Ten Days" (Decena Trágica), with the backing of the US Embassy in Mexico. Soon after, Huerta has Madero and his vice president assassinated.

March 1913: The Constitutionalists are formed, under the leadership of Venustiano Carranza, a landlord and the governor of Coahuila. They issue the Plan de Guadalupe, which calls for Huerta's ouster but, in line with Carranza's relative conservatism, makes no mention of agrarian or social reform. Álvaro Obregón, a man with past experience as a pro-Madero militia leader, joins the Constitutionalists in Sonora and eventually becomes a general under Carranza's command.

March 1913: Villa returns to Mexico with a small band of fighters. A few months later he will command the Constitutionalists' Northern Division, the most feared and powerful army in Mexico. Although nominally subordinate to Carranza, Villa chafes at Carranza's authority and disagrees with his conservative stance on agrarian and social questions.

May 1913: The Casa del Obrero Mundial, a new labor federation, calls the first major May Day demonstration in Mexican history.

1913–14: The Constitutionalist forces—especially the Northern Division—score multiple victories against the Federal Army.

April 1914: The Woodrow Wilson administration, in an effort to influence events in Mexico, orders US naval forces to attack and occupy the Gulf Coast city of Veracruz.

July 1914: Huerta resigns the presidency and flees Mexico. Carranza and his Constitutionalist forces take Mexico City. The old Federal Army is abolished.

July–October 1914: The tensions between Villa and Carranza come to the surface. Zapata continues to disavow Carranza's authority, due to Carranza's opposition to land reform. Villa eventually declares himself and the Northern Division to be independent of Carranza's command.

October–November 1914: The revolutionary military officers gather at the Aguascalientes Convention to settle their differences and decide the future of Mexico. Carranza holds firmly to the position that he should be president of Mexico. Yet the Convention swings to Villa and Zapata's side and declares its support for agrarian and social reform. Carranza is eventually declared to be in rebellion against the Convention.

November 1914: Carranza and his followers, including Obregón, leave Mexico City and retreat to Veracruz. US troops end their occupation.

December 1914: Villa and Zapata meet for the first time, and their forces enter Mexico City. The Convention establishes a government in the capital. Villa and Zapata soon return to their home bases in Chihuahua and Morelos.

January 1915: Under pressure from Obregón, Carranza issues his own agrarian and social reform program.

February 1915: Obregón retakes Mexico City, following Villa and Zapata's departure from the capital. Obregón forms an alliance with the Casa del Obrero Mundial, recruiting thousands of urban workers into his army.

April–June 1915: Obregón faces Villa in several major battles in the center-north Bajío region. Villa and the Northern Division are decisively defeated. Villa returns to the terrain of guerrilla warfare.

July 1915: Carranza returns to Mexico City and assumes the presidency of Mexico.

1915–19: Carranza's forces do battle with Zapata's increasingly isolated forces in Morelos but are unable to fully suppress the Zapatistas.

March 1916: Following numerous guerrilla raids in Chihuahua, Villa crosses the US-Mexico border and attacks Columbus, New Mexico, provoking an armed expedition by US troops in pursuit of him.

July 1916: The Casa del Obrero Mundial calls a general strike in Mexico City, demanding that workers be paid in gold rather than paper currency. Carranza's government puts down the strike by force.

December 1916–February 1917: Delegates in Querétaro draft Mexico's 1917 Constitution. Radicals in the Constitutionalist camp enshrine numerous social reforms in the final version, against Carranza's wishes.

April 1919: Zapata is killed by treachery, when meeting a Constitutionalist officer who claimed he wished to join forces with him.

June 1919: A disgruntled Obregón announces his presidential candidacy, against Carranza's wishes. Obregón receives the backing of Zapata's followers and the trade unions. Carranza instead declares his support for one of his own close loyalists.

April 1920: Facing charges of treason brought by Carranza's government, Obregón rebels and receives widespread backing from the Constitutionalist army.

May 1920: Carranza flees to Veracruz but is killed en route.

June 1920: A caretaker president reaches a peace agreement with Villa.

December 1920: Obregón assumes the presidency of Mexico.

Acknowledgments

This book has benefited from conversations and comments—critical and encouraging, and often both—from numerous individuals. Others have affected the direction of this project without knowing they did so. I would like to thank Anthony Arnove, Aurel de Coloblo Mendoza, Shane Dillingham, Samuel Farber, Sarah Hines, Giada Mangiameli, Bill and Barbara Myers, Michal Elaine Myers, Kate O'Neil, Colby Ristow, Gillian Russom, Lance Selfa, Mayra Terrones, and Jeffery Webber for a combination of their time, interest, and friendship.

I have also benefited over the years from the guidance of excellent teachers on matters related to Mexico and Latin America more broadly. Here I should take the opportunity to thank Reid Andrews, Dain Borges, Sydney Chalhoub, Douglas Cope, Anani Dzidzienyo, Alejandro de la Fuente, the late Friedrich Katz, Emilio Kouri, Agnes Lugo-Ortiz, Joshua Lund, Laura Putnam, and Mauricio Tenorio. Seymour Drescher and Jonathan Scott are not scholars of Latin America, but merit thanks as well.

Thanks also to the staff at Haymarket Books, and particularly Julie Fain, for helping guide the text to completion.

This book is dedicated to my parents, who made me who I am. Much love and thanks to you both, for everything.

Notes

Note that the suggestions for further reading included in this section are not meant to be an exhaustive survey of the scholarship on a given topic; they are provided for the reader interested in additional details on the issue at hand.

1. Setting the Stage

1. According to historian Adolfo Gilly, the "official history" of the Revolution merely asserts that "everyone was a good guy, and it [is] totally unclear why they all ended up killing each other." "Adolfo Gilly, Interview: 'What exists cannot be true,'" *New Left Review* 64 (July–August 2010): 41. The image used in this sentence should be credited to the late Friedrich Katz, who often made use of it.

2. Andrés Manuel López Obrador, "Con una insurgencia cívica y un despertar ciudadano se logrará la transformación del país y establecerá una auténtica y verdadera democracia: AMLO," November 20, 2010, available

at the Gobierno Legítimo de México website, www.amlo.org.mx.

3. Jorge Ramos, "Roger Bartra: Necesario 'enterrar' a la Revolución," *El Universal*, online edition, November 21, 2009.

4. On this history of revolt see Friedrich Katz, "Rural Rebellions after 1810," in Friedrich Katz, ed., *Riot, Rebellion, and Revolution: Rural Social Conflict in Mexico* (Princeton, NJ: Princeton University Press, 1988); John Coatsworth, "Patterns of Rural Rebellion in Latin America: Mexico in Comparative Perspective," in ibid.; and Alan Knight, "The Peculiarities of Mexican History: Mexico Compared to Latin America, 1821–1992,"*Journal of Latin American Studies* 24 (1992).

5. Further details on Mexico's economic transformation in this period can be found in Héctor Aguilar Camín and Lorenzo Meyer, *In the Shadow of the Mexican Revolution: Contemporary Mexican History, 1910–1989*, trans. Luis Alberto Fierro (Austin: University of Texas Press, 1993), 1–11; Adolfo Gilly, *The Mexican Revolution*, trans. Patrick Camiller (London: Verso, 1983), 28–37; Alan Knight, *Mexican Revolution*, vol. 1, *Porfirians, Liberals, and Peasants* (Lincoln: University of Nebraska Press, 1986), 80–81, and vol. 2, *Counter-revolution and Reconstruction*, 11–13; and Ramon Eduardo Ruíz, *The Great Rebellion: Mexico, 1905–1924* (New York: W. W. Norton, 1982), 9–19. On the role of foreign interests in particular see John Mason Hart, *Revolutionary Mexico: The Coming and Process of the Mexican Revolution* (Berkeley, University of California Press, 1987), 129–62, and Friedrich Katz, *The Secret War in Mexico: Europe, the United States, and the Mexican Revolution* (Chicago: University of Chicago Press, 1981), 21–27.

6. Gilly, *Mexican Revolution*, 45.

7. Knight, *Mexican Revolution*, 1:93, 121.

8. Cited in ibid., 1:26.

9. For more on the Porfirian *jefes políticos*, see ibid., 1:24–32.

10. Salvador Alvarado, cited in Aguilar Camín and Meyer, *In the Shadow of the Mexican Revolution*, 6.

11. For more on this tradition of grassroots or "popular" Liberalism, see Peter Guardino, "Barbarism or Republican Law? Guerrero's Peasants and National Politics, 1820–1846," *Hispanic American Historical Review* 75, no. 2 (May 1995); Knight, *Mexican Revolution*, 1:162–24, 309–12; Florencia Mallon, *Peasant and Nation: The Making of Postcolonial Mexico and Peru* (Berkeley: University of California Press, 1995), chap. 2; and

Guy Thompson, "Popular Aspects of Liberalism in Mexico, 1848–1888," *Bulletin of Latin American Research* 10, no. 3 (1991).

12. The historian Alan Knight has coined the term *"serrano* revolt" to refer to this phenomenon. For more detail see Alan Knight, "Peasant and Caudillo in Revolutionary Mexico," in David Brading, ed., *Caudillo and Peasant in the Mexican Revolution* (Cambridge: Cambridge University Press, 1980).

13. For more on the particular character of the Mexican north, see Barry Carr, *The Peculiarities of the Mexican North, 1880–1928: An Essay in Interpretation* (Glasgow: University of Glasgow, 1971); Katz, *Secret War in Mexico*, 7–21; Friedrich Katz, *The Life and Times of Pancho Villa* (Stanford, CA: Stanford University Press, 1998), 11–56; Knight, *The Mexican Revolution*, 1:42; and John Tutino, *From Insurrection to Revolution in Mexico* (Princeton, NJ: Princeton University Press, 1989), 297–305.

14. For more on the Liberal clubs and prerevolutionary Liberals, see James Cockroft, *Intellectual Precursors of the Mexican Revolution, 1900–1913* (Austin: University of Texas Press, 1976). For a different perspective, see Knight, *Mexican Revolution*, 1:44–47, 229–30.

15. Aguilar Camín and Meyer, *In the Shadow of the Mexican Revolution*, 6. See also Knight, *Mexican Revolution*, 1:35.

16. See Knight, *Mexican Revolution*, 1:79.

17. Knight, *Mexican Revolution*, 1:104. For another example of this sort see Mallon, *Peasant and Nation*, 137–38.

18. Tutino, *From Insurrection to Revolution in Mexico*, 281.

19. For more details on how this process of land privatization was carried out (or attempted) in different parts of Mexico, see Charles Berry, "The Fiction and Fact of the Reform: The Case of the Central District of Oaxaca, 1856–1867," *The Americas* 26, no. 3 (January 1970); Knight, *Mexican Revolution*, 1:94–115; Emilio Kourí, *A Pueblo Divided: Business, Property, and Community in Papantla, Mexico* (Stanford, CA: Stanford University Press, 2004), esp. chaps. 3–6; Jennie Purnell, "'With All Due Respect': Popular Resistance to the Privatization of Communal Lands in Nineteenth-Century Michoacán," *Latin American Research Review* 34, no. 1 (1999); Guy Thomson, "Agrarian Conflict in the Municipality of Cuetzalan (Sierra de Puebla): The Rise and Fall of 'Pala' Agustin Dieguillo, 1861–1894," *Hispanic American Historical Review* 71, no. 2 (May 1991).

20. Knight, *Mexican Revolution*, 1:95, 111.
21. Arnaldo Córdova, *La ideología de la Revolución Mexicana: La formación del nuevo régimen* (Mexico City: Ediciones Era, 1973), 156.
22. Knight, *Mexican Revolution*, 1:96.
23. Cited in David W. Walker, "Homegrown Revolution: The Hacienda Santa Catalina del Alamo y Anexas and Agrarian Protest in Eastern Durango, Mexico, 1897–1913," *Hispanic American Historical Review* 72, no. 2 (May 1992): 249.
24. For more details on conditions for hacienda peones and tenants in various regions of Mexico see Friedrich Katz, "Labor Conditions on Haciendas in Porfirian Mexico: Some Trends and Tendencies," *Hispanic American Historical Review* 54, no. 1 (February 1974); Knight, *Mexican Revolution*, 1:85–92; Tutino, *From Insurrection to Revolution in Mexico*, 288–321; Walker, "Homegrown Revolution"; Arturo Warman, *"We Come to Object": The Peasants of Morelos and the National State*, trans. Stephen K. Ault (Baltimore: Johns Hopkins University Press, 1980), 55–61.
25. Warman, *"We Come to Object,"* 107.
26. For more on hacienda tenants in particular, see Knight, *Mexican Revolution*, 1:91–92; Tutino, *From Insurrection to Revolution in Mexico*, 305–15; Walker, "Homegrown Revolution," 248–50.
27. Cited in Knight, *Mexican Revolution*, 1:92.
28. The story of the village of Naranja in this period is told in Paul Friedrich, *Agrarian Revolt in a Mexican Village* (Englewood Cliffs, NJ: Prentice-Hall, 1970).
29. Dudley Ankerson, *Agrarian Warlord: Saturnino Cedillo and the Mexican Revolution in San Luis Potosí* (DeKalb: Northern Illinois University Press, 1984), 11.
30. John Womack, *Zapata and the Mexican Revolution* (New York: Vintage, 1970), 44; Knight, *Mexican Revolution*, 1:95–96.
31. Cited in Katz, *Life and Times of Pancho Villa*, 74.
32. Cited in Womack, *Zapata and the Mexican Revolution*, 63.
33. For more on these issues see T. G. Powell, "Mexican Intellectuals and the Indian Question, 1876–1911," *Hispanic American Historical Review* 48, no. 1 (February 1968); and Martin Stabb, "Indigenism and Racism in Mexican Thought, 1957–1911," *Journal of Inter-American Studies* 1, no. 4 (October 1959).
34. Warman, *"We Come to Object,"* 53.

35. Cited in Knight, *Mexican Revolution*, 1:286.
36. For more on these changes see Rodney Anderson, *Outcasts in Their Own Land: Mexican Industrial Workers, 1906–1911* (DeKalb: Northern Illinois University Press, 1976), chap. 2.
37. Knight, *Mexican Revolution*, 131.
38. On Mexican workers and Liberalism, see Anderson, *Outcasts in Their Own Land*, 312–26; Knight, *Mexican Revolution*, 137–39; and John Lear, *Workers, Neighbors, and Citizens: The Revolution in Mexico City* (Lincoln: University of Nebraska Press, 2001), 129–33.
39. For more on working conditions in Porfirian Mexico see Anderson, *Outcasts in Their Own Land*, p. 50–61.
40. For more on urban workers' living conditions in this period see ibid., 43–45.

2. 1910–1914

1. Cited in Knight, *Mexican Revolution*, 1:389.
2. Cited in ibid., 1:59.
3. Cited in Aguilar Camín and Meyer, *In the Shadow of the Mexican Revolution*, 1.
4. Lear, *Workers, Neighbors, and Citizens*, 129.
5. On urban workers' participation in the Madero campaign, see Anderson, *Outcasts in Their Own Land*, 57–8, 69–70, and Lear, *Workers, Neighbors, and Citizens*, 128–36.
6. Cited in Knight, *Mexican Revolution*, 1:188, 196.
7. Cited in ibid., 1:216.
8. Cited in Ruiz, *Great Rebellion*, 219.
9. Knight, *Mexican Revolution*, 1:232.
10. Womack, *Zapata and the Mexican Revolution*, 87.
11. For more detail on these and other incidents of rural revolt and violence, see ibid., 1:218–27, 331–51.
12. Ibid., 1:414.
13. Womack, *Zapata and the Mexican Revolution*, 93.
14. Cited in Gilly, *Mexican Revolution*, 73.
15. Cited in Aguilar Camín and Meyer, *In the Shadow of the Mexican Revolution*, 16, 25; Knight, *Mexican Revolution*, 1:231, 2:417.

16. Gilly, *Mexican Revolution*, 77.
17. Cited in Knight, *Mexican Revolution*, 1:228.
18. Cited in Gilly, *Mexican Revolution*, 89–90.
19. Ankerson, *Agrarian Warlord*, 58.
20. Knight, *Mexican Revolution*, 1:417, 460–61, 463–66.
21. Cited in Katz, *Secret War in Mexico*, 92.
22. Cited in Knight, *Mexican Revolution*, 1:285.
23. Cited in Katz, *Secret War in Mexico*, 94.
24. Cited in Knight, *Mexican Revolution*, 2:9.
25. "The cockroach, the cockroach / Can't walk anymore, / Because he lacks, because he doesn't have, / Marijuana to smoke." Many thanks to Dain Borges for this anecdote, and for his fine singing voice.
26. Cited in Katz, *Secret War in Mexico*, 120.
27. Cited in Knight, *Mexican Revolution*, 2:490.
28. Alan Knight's apt description, from *Mexican Revolution*, 2:112.
29. Katz, *Secret War in Mexico*, 145.
30. Elena Poniatowska, *Las Soldaderas: Women of the Mexican Revolution*, trans. David Dorado Romo (El Paso: Cinco Puntos, 14). See also Elizabeth Salas, *Soldaderas in the Mexican Military: Myth and History* (Austin: University of Texas Press, 1990), chaps. 3–5.
31. Cited in Katz, *Secret War in Mexico*, 187.
32. Cited in ibid., 150. For more on the US government's evolving views of both Villa and Carranza see ibid., chap. 8.

3. 1914–1920

1. Cited in Gilly, *Mexican Revolution*, 129.
2. Cited in Romana Falcón, "San Luis Potosí: Confiscated Estates—Revolutionary Conquest or Spoils?" in Thomas Benjamin and Mark Wasserman, eds., *Provinces of the Revolution: Essays on Regional Mexican History, 1910–1929* (Albuquerque: University of New Mexico Press, 1990), 153.
3. Cited in Gilly, *Mexican Revolution*, 129.
4. Ibid., 130.
5. Ibid., 141.
6. Ankerson, *Agrarian Warlord*, 58–59, 68–70.

7. On Contreras and Durango, see Pedro Salmerón Sanginés, "Lucha agraria y revolución en el oriente de Durango (1900–1929)," *Historia Mexicana* 56, no. 1 (July September 2006); and Walker, "Homegrown Revolution."

8. On Carrera Torres, see Heather Fowler Salamini, "Tamaulipas: Land Reform and the State," in Benjamin and Wasserman, eds., *Provinces of the Revolution*; Ankerson, *Agrarian Warlord*, 67, 71. On Arenas, see Raymond Th. J. Buvé, "Peasant Movements, Caudillos and Land Reform during the Revolution (1910–1917) in Tlaxcala," *Boletín de Estudios Latinoamericanos y del Caribe* 18 (June 1975): esp. 143–46; on Salgado, see Ian Jacobs, *Ranchero Revolt: The Mexican Revolution in Guerrero* (Austin: University of Texas Press, 1982), chap. 5.

9. For two examples of this phenomenon from the states of Guerrero and Hidalgo, see Jacobs, *Ranchero Revolt*, esp. chap. 5, and Frans Schryer, *The Rancheros of Pisaflores: The History of a Peasant Bourgeoisie in Twentieth-Century Mexico* (Toronto: University of Toronto Press, 1980), esp. chap. 4.

10. Gilly, *Mexican Revolution*, 184.

11. Lear, *Workers, Neighbors, and Citizens*, 262.

12. Katz, *Secret War in Mexico*, 125.

13. Knight, *Mexican Revolution*, 2:304.

14. This basic observation should be credited to Córdova, *Ideología de la Revolución Mexicana*, 144.

15. Katz, *Secret War in Mexico*, 127. For more on these differences see ibid., 123–28, 139–42, and Knight, *Mexican Revolution*, 1:304–06.

16. Cited in Knight, *Mexican Revolution*, 2:516.

17. This distinction is drawn in part from ibid., 2:128–29.

18. Cited in ibid., 2:315.

19. Lear, *Workers, Neighbors, and Citizens*, 256, 269.

20. For more on the origins of the Casa see ibid., 171–80.

21. Cited in Knight, *Mexican Revolution*, 1:441.

22. Cited in ibid., 2:318.

23. For more on the emergence of the alliance between the Casa and the Constitutionalists, see Lear, *Workers, Neighbors, and Citizens*, 246–88.

24. For examples of the reaction of workers outside the Casa to Obregón's policies, see ibid., 276.

25. For more on this growth of working-class political engagement, see Anderson, *Outcasts in Their Own Land*, 242–72; Lear, *Workers, Neighbors,*

and Citizens, chaps. 3–4 and pp. 180–83, 281–83.

26. See for example Gilly, *Mexican Revolution,* chap. 10.
27. Lear, *Workers, Neighbors, and Citizens,* 190, 255, 276.
28. Ibid., 274.
29. On the nature of grassroots or "popular" anticlericalism, see Knight, *Mexican Revolution,* 2:202–08, and Lear, *Workers, Neighbors, and Citizens,* 260–62, 284–78. See also Alan Knight, "Popular Culture and the Revolutionary State in Mexico, 1910–1940," *Hispanic American Historical Review* 74, no. 3 (August 1994): esp. 426–41.
30. For this critique of the Red Batallions' relative significance in the short term, see Knight, *Mexican Revolution,* 2:320–21, and Lear, *Workers, Neighbors, and Citizens,* 288–89.
31. See for example Gilly, *Mexican Revolution,* 182.
32. Cited in ibid., 162.
33. Cited in Knight, *Mexican Revolution,* 2:322.
34. For more on this see Katz, *Secret War in Mexico,* 298–307.
35. Katz, *Life and Times of Pancho Villa,* 633–35.
36. Cited in Ruiz, *Great Rebellion,* 215.
37. Cited in ibid., 246.
38. Katz, *Secret War in Mexico,* 271.
39. Cited in Katz, *Life and Times of Pancho Villa,* 617.
40. Falcón, "San Luis Potosí," in Benjamin and Wasserman, *Provinces of Revolution,* 154.
41. For more on the transformation of generals into landlords see ibid.; Katz, *Secret War in Mexico,* 147–78, 253–58; and Ruiz, *Great Rebellion,* chap. 15.
42. Cited in Ruiz, *Great Rebellion,* 250.
43. Cited in Córdova, *Ideología de la Revolución Mexicana,* 213.
44. Cited in Gilly, *Mexican Revolution,* 218.
45. Womack, *Zapata and the Mexican Revolution,* 170.
46. Cited in Knight, *Mexican Revolution,* 2:363.
47. Ibid., 366.
48. This is a paraphrase of sorts of a point made by John Tutino: "While agrarian insurgents could not win, many would not lose." Tutino, *From Insurrection to Revolution in Mexico,* 337.
49. The original title in Spanish of his book *The Mexican Revolution* is *La revolución interrumpida* (the interrupted revolution).

50. See Ruiz, *Great Rebellion*, 252–53.
51. Cited in Gilly, *Mexican Revolution*, 22.
52. Cited in Córdova, *Ideología de la Revolución Mexicana*, 210–11.
53. Cited in ibid., 270.
54. Ruiz, *Great Rebellion*, 299.
55. This observation should be credited to Alan Knight, from "The Peculiarities of Mexican History: Mexico Compared to Latin America, 1821–1992," *Journal of Latin American Studies* 24, suppl. S1, *The Colonial and Post Colonial Experience: Five Centuries of Spanish and Portuguese America* (Cambridge: Cambridge University Press, 1992), 99–144.
56. Ruiz, *Great Rebellion*, 334–35.

Index

Page numbers in *italics* refer to illustrations. Passim (literally scattered) indicates intermittent discussion of a topic over a cluster of pages.

Agrarian Party, 136
Agua Prieta, Sonora, 125
Aguascalientes Convention (1914), 93–122 passim, 129
Alvarado, Salvador, 108, 128, 135, 139
AMLO, 2, 4
Anenecuilco, Morelos, 50–51
Ángeles, Felipe, 106, 123
Anti-Reelectionist Party, 46
Apaches, 50
Arango, José Doroteo. *See* Villa, Pancho
Arenas, Domingo, 89, 132, 134
Aztecs, 50–51

Bajío, 121
Bartra, Roger, 2–3, 4

Blanco, Lucio, 86–87, 94
Britain. *See* Great Britain

Caballero, Luis, 128
Cabrera, Luis, 53
Cananea, Sonora, 6–7, 36, 37
Cárdenas, Lázaro, 141–42
Carranza, Venustiano, 1–3 passim, 38, 39, *69*, 78–109 passim, 116–19 passim, 125–37 passim
    death, 38, 137
    home state, 13, 68
    repression by, 131–32
    rise, 68–71
    Villa relations, 70–71, 83–86 passim, 90–93 passim, 99–100, 105, 106, 125
    Zapata relations, 70, 84–88 passim, 93–94, 130
Carrera Torres, Alberto, 89, 132
Carrera Torres, Francisco, 89
Casa del Obrero Mundial, 114–20, 131, 132
Castro, Jesús Agustín, 108

Catholic Church, 70, 114, 119, 120, 129
Cedillo, Saturnino, 136
Cedillo family, 25–26, 88–89, 136
Chiapas, 108
Chihuahua, 13, 48–50, 68
  Constitutionalists in, 110, 125
  Huerta repression in, 67
  land confiscation in, 90–92 passim, 106
  taxation in, 9–10
  Villa base and action in, 1, 9–10, 71–78 passim, 90–92, 99–100, 105, 125–27, 137–38
  Villa death in, 140
  wealthy landowners in, 18, 48
Chihuahua City, 77, 99, 100
China (person). *See* La China
Ciudadela, 64, 65
Ciudad Juárez, 52
Ciudad México. *See* Mexico City
Coahuila, 13, 24, 34, 68, 88, 138
Constitutionalists, 69–71, 78–86 passim, 92–95 passim, 104, 108, 109, 117–35 passim. *See also* Aguascalientes Convention (1914)
Constitution of 1857, 14, 46, 69, 129
Constitution of 1917, 2, 129, 135
Contreras, Calixto, 89, 132
Creelman, James, 44
Cuautla, Morelos, 52
"La cucaracha" (song), 66, 158n24
Cuernavaca, Morelos, 52

Decena Trágica, 64–65, *65*, 119
De la O, Genovevo, 88, 134

Diáz, Felix, 63–64
Díaz, Porfirio, 4–18 passim, *5, 6*, 26–63 passim, 103, 129
  exile and death, 52
  presidential campaign of 1910, 41–47 passim
Díaz Soto y Gama, Antonio, 94, 121, 136
Durango, 22, 24, 26, 28–29, 48, 89, 137

"Embassy Pact," 63
Espinosa y Parra family, 87

France, 7

Germany, 66
Gilly, Adolfo, 59, 88, 97, 138–39, 153n1
González, Abraham, 66–67
Great Britain, 7
Guadalupe, Virgin of. *See* Virgin of Guadalupe
Guajardo, Jésus, 133, 137
Guanajuato, 124
Guanajuato (city), 9
Guerrero, 54, 90, 132

Hearst, William Randolph, 18
Hidalgo, 26, 55
Huerta, Victoriano, 61–72 passim, *67*, 86–92 passim, 97–99 passim, 106, 119
  army relations, 76
  Casa del Obrero Mundial relations, 115–16
  Catholic Church aid to, 114

resignation and self-exile, 80, 83
US relations, 77–78
Villa relations, 71–72
Hueyapan, Morelos, 28

Iguapalapa, Guerrero, 54–55
Institutional Revolutionary Party
(PRI). *See* PRI

Jockey Club, 116, 131
Juárez. *See* Ciudad Juárez

Katz, Friedrich, 74, 104, 107, 153n1
Knight, Alan, 56, 104–5, 135

La China, 134
Laguna, 23–24, 30, 54, 62, 89, 132
Lear, John, 119
Limantour, José, 42
López Obrador, Andrés Manuel. *See*
AMLO

Madero, Francisco, 1–2, 40–71 passim, *42*, 76, 86–89 passim, 95
deposition and execution, 65, 67, 77
home state, 13
middle-class support, 15
presidential campaign of 1910, 37,
40–47 passim, *43*
presidential election of 1911, 52
repression by, 59–62
upper-class relations, 61–63 passim, 97, 98
working-class relations, 37, 62,
115, 118
Zapata support, 38
Madero, Gustavo, 64, 66

Mapimi Bulge, 138
Mexican Telephone and Telegraph
Company, 116–17
Mexico City, 12, 34–35, *35*, 64–65,
101–5 passim
dire conditions (1915), 127
general strikes, 131
Obregón in, 114–21
Villa and Zapata in, 71, 101, 102,
104–5, 109–13, 120–22 passim
Michoacán, 25, 26, 55
Morelos, 1, 56–62 passim, 68, 85,
103–5 passim, 110, 113, 120–23
passim
commercial agriculture in, 24
landlords in, 27, 56
land occupation and repossession,
51, 54, 88, 90, 98, 120
population decline (1918), 132
post-Zapata, 133–34
villages, 26, 28, 50–51, 59, 60, 74,
141
Zapata victory over Federal Army
in, 52
Morones, Luis, 117, 136
Múgica, Francisco, 108, 128, 129
Mutual Film Company, 78

Nahuatl, 50–51
Namiquipa, Chihuahua, 126
Naranja, Michoacán, 25, 26
New Mexico, 127
Nuevo Léon, 45

Obregón, Álvaro, 1–2, 38, 84–86,
92–93, 96–128 passim, *97*, *98*,

136–38

Obregón (cont.)
home state, 13
presidential election of 1920, 137
repression by, 140
Villa relations, 99–101, 117, 121–22, 138

Orizaba, 36

Palafox, Manuel, 94, 121, 132–33
Parral, Chihuahua, 140
Party of the Institutionalized Revolution (PRI). See PRI
Pino Suárez, José María, 67–68
Plan de Ayala, 3–4, 58–59, 70, 74, 87–90 passim, 94, 106, 133
Plan de Guadalupe, 69, 86
Plan de San Luis Potosí, 47–48
Poniatowska, Elena, 76
PRI, 3, 142
Puebla, 36, 89, 141
Puebla (city), 122

Querétaro, 17, 129

Revolutionary Junta for Aid to the Public, 114
Reyes, Bernardo, 45–46, 63–64
Ricault, Alfredo, 128
Richardson Construction Company, 18
Río Blanco, Veracruz, 37
Russian Revolution (1917), 121

Sabinas, Coahuila, 138
Salgado, Jesús, 90, 132
San Antonio, Texas, 47

San José de Gracia, Durango, 26
San Luis Potosí, 18, 25–26, 61, 87, 88, 89, 130
San Luis Potosí (city), 47
San Pablo Oztotepec, 3
Santa Rosalía, Chihuahua, 126
Sonora, 13, 37, 68, 69, 99, 125, 134

Tabasco, 108
Taft, William Howard, 63
Tamaulipas, 86, 89, 132
Tampico, Tamaulipas, 79–80, 109
Ten Tragic Days. See Decena Trágica
Tepalcingo, Morelos, 26
Tequisquitengo, Morelos, 26
Terrazas, Luis, 18, 19, 48, 72, 74, 91, 130
Terrazas family, 10
Tlaxcala, 89, 132, 134
Torreón, 30, 52, 54
Torreón Pact, 92, 93
Tutino, John, 17

United Kingdom. See Great Britain
United States, 45, 70, 77–80, 101
Cárdenas relations, 142
Carranza relations, 78, 125, 127
Díaz relations, 37
Huerta relations, 66, 70, 77
investors and investment, 7, 18, 130
Madero in, 47
Madero relations, 63
occupation of Veracruz, 78–80, 79, 101
press, 44
Villa relations, 77–78, 126–27

Vasconcelos, José, 112–13
Veracruz, 36, 37, 78–79, *79*, 101, 134,
   137, 141
Villa, Pancho, 1–2, 38, 48–52 passim, *50, 73*, 72–127 passim, *91*,
   137–38
   assassination, 140
   brutality of, 126
   Carranza relations, 70–71, 83–86
      passim, 90–93 passim, 99–
      100, 105, 106, 125
   followers, 34, 68
   home state, 9–10, 48
   Huerta relations, 71–72
   Obregón relations, 99–101, 117,
      121–22, 138
   prison escape, 71–72
   US relations, 77–78, 126–27
Villa de Carbonera, San Luis Potosí,
   25–26
Virgin of Guadalupe, 120

Warman, Arturo, 23
Western Federation of Miners, 36
Wilson, Henry Lane, 63, 64
Wilson, Woodrow, 77–80
Womack, John, 54, 56

Xochimilco, 101

Yaquis, 134, 140
Yucatán, 10, 34, 55, 108, 109, 139

Zacatecas, 18
Zapata, Emiliano, 1–2, 38, 51–61
   passim, *52, 58*, 74, 83–123 passim, *123*
Carranza relations, 70, 84–88 passim, 93–94, 130
grassroots social base, 3, 39, 75
last days and assassination, 132–33
press coverage, 60
support of Madero, 38
Zapata, Eufemio, 57, 132

About Haymarket Books

Haymarket Books is a nonprofit, progressive book distributor and publisher, a project of the Center for Economic Research and Social Change. We believe that activists need to take ideas, history, and politics into the many struggles for social justice today. Learning the lessons of past victories, as well as defeats, can arm a new generation of fighters for a better world. As Karl Marx said, "The philosophers have merely interpreted the world; the point, however, is to change it."

We take inspiration and courage from our namesakes, the Haymarket Martyrs, who gave their lives fighting for a better world. Their 1886 struggle for the eight-hour day reminds workers around the world that ordinary people can organize and struggle for their own liberation.

For more information and to shop our complete catalog of titles, visit us online at www.haymarketbooks.org.

Also from Haymarket Books

American Insurgents: A Brief History of American Anti-Imperialism
Richard Seymour

From Rebellion to Reform in Bolivia: Class Struggle, Indigenous Liberation, and the Politics of Evo Morales • Jeffery R. Webber

How Revolutionary Were the Bourgeois Revolutions? • Neil Davidson

History of the Russian Revolution • Leon Trotsky

On History: Tariq Ali and Oliver Stone in Conversation
Tariq Ali and Oliver Stone

Revolution in Seattle: A Memoir • Harvey O'Connor

Printed in the USA
CPSIA information can be obtained
at www.ICGtesting.com
JSHW052154081023
49665JS00004B/5